I0019488

Outsourcing Technical Writing

A Primer

Barry Saiff

Outsourcing Technical Writing

A Primer

Copyright © 2018 Barry Saiff

All rights reserved. No part of this book may be reproduced or transmitted in any form or by any means without the prior written permission of the copyright holder, except for the inclusion of brief quotations in a review.

Disclaimer

The information in this book is provided on an "as is" basis, without warranty. While every effort has been taken by the author and XML Press in the preparation of this book, the author and XML Press shall have neither liability nor responsibility to any person or entity with respect to any loss or damages arising from the information contained herein.

This book contains links to third-party web sites that are not under the control of the author or XML Press. The author and XML Press are not responsible for the content of any linked site. Inclusion of a link in this book does not imply that the author or XML Press endorses or accepts any responsibility for the content of that third-party site.

Credits

Series Producer and Editor:	Scott Abel
Series Cover Design:	Marc Posch
Publisher:	Richard Hamilton

Trademarks

XML Press and the XML Press logo are trademarks of XML Press.

All terms mentioned in this book that are known to be trademarks or service marks have been capitalized as appropriate. Use of a term in this book should not be regarded as affecting the validity of any trademark or service mark.

XML Press
Laguna Hills, California
http://xmlpress.net

First Edition
ISBN: 978-1-937434-64-9 (print)
ISBN: 978-1-937434-65-6 (ebook)

Table of Contents

Preface

Are you afraid of outsourcing your technical writing? If so, perhaps it's because you believe one or more of the following things about outsourcing technical writing:

- Outsourcing always leads to reduced content quality.
- Outsourcing always results in layoffs.
- Outsourcing always reduces morale on existing teams.
- Outsourcing can usually cut costs by more than 60%.

All of these statements are false. Are you surprised?

This book provides a comprehensive introduction to technical writing outsourcing. In the following pages, you will learn that:

- Outsourcing can lead to increased content quality.
- Outsourcing often does not result in any layoffs.
- Outsourcing can actually boost morale on existing writing teams.
- Outsourcing can rarely, if ever, reduce content development costs by more than 60%.

In addition to outsourcing technical writing and other types of content development, this book also discusses management and the keys to organizational effectiveness.

Why discuss management in a book about technical writing outsourcing? Effective management is a prerequisite for effective outsourcing. If your management practices are not adequate for your current situation, outsourcing is likely to exacerbate your challenges.

> If you want to understand how to create positive results from outsourcing, you need to first understand how to create positive results in business more broadly.

Who should read this book?

If you are a technical communications professional – whether an individual contributor or a manager – you will likely not have sole authority over decisions to outsource, and you may not even get advance notice before outsourcing occurs. The key question for you is not whether to outsource, but how to most effectively outsource.

Your interest in this book shows that you are already ahead of the game. By learning about outsourcing, you can move from fear to mastery. You can prepare yourself to influence outsourcing decisions before they happen and help ensure that the results are positive.

Lead writers, managers, and related decision makers

If you're in one of these categories and you're not involved in outsourcing yet, you will be soon. Read this book to prepare yourself. Each of the chapters contains information that you will find useful at some point in your outsourcing journey.

Outsourcing professionals

If you work in procurement, purchasing, vendor management, or outsourcing management, you may not be familiar with technical communicators. Read this book to learn about the specific challenges involved in outsourcing content development.

For decision makers and outsourcing professionals, this book answers the following questions:

- Is outsourcing right for your organization?
- What key factors must you consider at each stage of the outsourcing process?
- What does it take to succeed in outsourcing technical writing?
- What are the keys to organizational effectiveness, and how can management contribute to the success of an outsourcing effort?

Technical writers

If you are a technical writer, your job security depends on a variety of factors – some within and some outside your control. Fear and resistance to outsourcing will not help you advance. On the contrary, they can lead you to miss opportunities. By embracing the reality of outsourcing, you can prepare yourself to take advantage of the changes coming your way. Check out the section titled "Adjusting to outsourcing as a team member" in Chapter 14 for guidance on adopting a healthy mindset and explore some of the other chapters to understand the pressures and trade-offs facing your management team as they make decisions about outsourcing.

For technical writers, this book answers the following questions:

- If you are not making all the decisions, how can you best deal with the changes that outsourcing brings?
- How can you continue to contribute to, and be valued by, your organization?

A personal note

Before getting involved in technical writing outsourcing, I had a long career in technical documentation. I started as a technical writer in 1984. Over the next 26 years, I led documentation teams at six companies, sometimes creating teams from scratch. For the first 25 of those years, I worked exclusively with technical writers based in the United States. Other departments – particularly software engineering and quality assurance – sometimes had offshore members, but never the technical writing team. In my final year working in the US, that changed. I was working for a large software company, and our division had begun reducing staff in the US and expanding into India and China. That year, we added two writers in India.

At first, I was skeptical of the Indian writers. Their written English had grammar issues, and they made other mistakes. However, I soon discovered that they were amazing learners. If I explained what was wrong with their text, they would fix it, and they would not make the same mistakes again.

By this point, I had worked as a contract technical writer for much of my career. Typically, I worked full-time, on-site at a client company, but I was actually employed by a contracting firm. The contractor paid me an hourly wage with no benefits. Usually the hourly wage was higher than I could get as a salaried employee and sometimes the contractor facilitated my purchase of benefits.

One of the aspects of this situation that I liked was the freedom my employers had to get rid of me quickly. (Yes, you read that correctly.) If my work was not satisfactory, they could fire me. That didn't happen. Instead, I continued to get new contracts, at higher rates, often staying at a client company longer than most of the employees I worked with. I always knew that I was doing good work – because if I wasn't, the job would end.

The client paid the contractor an hourly rate for my work. This rate was significantly higher than the rate I actually received – anywhere from 33% to 100% higher. For years I thought, if only I could get into that business, I could make a great deal of money. However, I really didn't know how to get started, and it seemed that I would need a great deal of capital.

In 2004, I was working in-house for a startup when we were bought by a large, established software company. As Director of Documentation and someone who had started early at the firm, I had quite a few shares of stock. I realized that I did not have enough money to start a company in the US, but perhaps I had enough to start one in the Philippines.

Why the Philippines? Two primary reasons: first, English is one of the two official languages of the country. And second, given the country's long history with the United States, the culture is very Western-friendly.

So, in my last few years living and working in San Francisco, I began researching how it might work to build a technical writing outsourcing company in the Philippines. I talked with other documentation leaders and managers who worked on teams that were split between India and the US. I asked about their challenges.

The two primary issues with the writers in India were quality and turnover. Regarding quality, I asked about editing. Despite the fact that English was not the writers' native language, editing was often dropped from the budget. Turnover was also an issue due to the hot job market in Indian technology centers. However, I suspected that another cause of the high turnover rates might be management.

When I started my company, about a year after moving to the Philippines, I sought to address these issues. I did not start in one of the three major cities – Manila, Davao, or Cebu. Given the number of educated, skilled people throughout the Philippines, I had many good choices about where to begin. We launched our business in the mountain resort town of Tagaytay City, in the province of Cavite, adjacent to the National Capital Region. Seven years later, with a full-time staff of 75, we are still in Tagaytay City. People are grateful to find good jobs near where they live.

I also designed the company to address the quality issue. From the start, we were not just a company of Filipino technical writers. The company was owned and run by an experienced US technical communications leader (yours truly). I was also our first editor. We now have teams of quality control specialists, editors, and others who review content to ensure quality. We also employ a variety of remote consultants, in Europe, North America, and Asia. We've hired a team of multimedia artists and expanded our business into animation, video, and motion infographics, and we're starting to train our writing team in multimedia arts as well.

I've worked hard to build a good corporate culture, based on a set of values and basic commitments that include excellence, honesty, and integrity. We do not engage in deception. We treat people fairly. In seven years, we've had only five resignations.

Along the way, I've learned a great deal about how to make technical writing outsourcing work. Despite all the obstacles and challenges, our teams have made some of the largest companies in the world very happy. And crucially, none of our customers have been interested in saving money alone (though they certainly have saved a great deal). Year in and year out, we have been lucky to work with companies that care deeply about content quality.

Moreover, despite the frequency of layoffs involving outsourcing, layoffs have never occurred at our client companies as a result of our work.

And yet, what I've learned from working directly in technical writing outsourcing is not widely understood in the US technical communication community. Many technical writers are deeply threatened by the idea of outsourcing. They often have difficulty letting go of their assumptions that outsourcing always leads to reductions in quality – or worse, layoffs – even in the face of evidence to the contrary.

One thing that has contributed to my success is being attracted to reality. This hunger to find out the facts is fundamental to technical communicators. Up to this point, there has been no book that helps readers navigate the true challenges and opportunities of technical writing outsourcing. I'm proud to say that now there is.

How to use this book

This book is divided into four parts plus an appendix:

- Part I (Chapters 1 and 2) describes the rise of outsourcing, the forces behind it, and why outsourcing may be right for your company.
- Part II (Chapters 3 and 4) focuses on management and organizational effectiveness.
- Part III (Chapters 5 through 17) offers a roadmap for creating, selling, and implementing an outsourcing plan.
- Part IV (Chapters 18 and 19) contains case studies and some conclusions.
- Appendix: Sample Outsourcing Agreement

An Introduction to Outsourcing

CHAPTER 1
Introduction

Many people see outsourcing as a cause of disruption, dysfunction, organizational failure, and layoffs. While outsourcing can be followed by these things, consider the following:

- Outsourcing alone does not lead to layoffs, dysfunction, or other negative outcomes. Whether you have good or bad results depends primarily on *how* decisions are made and *how* outsourcing is planned and implemented
- The same factors that lead to negative outcomes from outsourcing also lead to bad business results more generally, even in the absence of outsourcing.

Outsourcing often gets blamed for things that actually have deeper causes. For example, if your organization has immature processes, outsourcing can exacerbate the resulting challenges. The following red flags are strong indications that your organization is not ready for outsourcing:

- Technical writers struggle to find out about user interface changes
- Product specifications are incomplete, out of date, or don't exist
- Subject matter experts have no time to answer writers' questions

Until you address these process deficiencies, outsourcing is unlikely to work and may make matters worse.

Sometimes, companies engage in outsourcing as a way to address internal disruption, dysfunction, or organizational failure. As we will see later, outsourcing under these conditions is likely to fail.

Understanding outsourcing

Regardless of whether you are responsible for planning or managing out-sourcing, you can benefit from understanding how it works. The following terms are important for understanding outsourcing:

- **In-house:** Work performed by the employees of an enterprise, generally in the enterprise's offices.
- **Outsourced:** Work performed by organizations or contractors external to the enterprise.
- **Onshore:** Work performed in the enterprise's home country or home region (Europe, North America, etc.).
- **Nearshore:** Work performed in other countries that are close to the home country in both location and cost of living – usually in either the same time zone or a close time zone.
- **Offshore:** Work performed in other countries, typically with large time zone differences and much lower labor costs.

Various combinations of these terms are possible (for example: in-house offshore or outsourced nearshore). In this book, I use the term outsourcing to mean outsourced offshore work.

Growth and drivers of technical writing outsourcing

While technical writing outsourcing is relatively new, outsourcing is not. For decades, quality assurance functions and computer programming work have been outsourced. Many of the best practices in these arenas also apply to technical writing.

Technical writing is a skill that cuts across industries and subject areas. Just as a Java-trained software engineer can create software for a variety of in-dustries, so can technical writers create clear, powerful content for clients across many industry sectors.

Ethical outsourcing

Unfortunately, outsourcing is often associated with some of its worst practices – especially the exploitation and mistreatment of labor. These are real problems in parts of the outsourcing world, and they must be taken very seriously.

However, there are outsourcing situations in which workers are treated well, paid a living wage, provided with good benefits, and offered extensive education, training, and advancement opportunities. These situations often compare favorably to in-house, onshore situations in which workers are underpaid, mistreated, or abused.

The economic forces behind outsourcing

Outsourcing is largely driven by cost-cutting pressures (competition, investors, etc.). If businesses can reduce costs while other factors remain stable, profits increase. And one of the surest ways to increase profits is to boost productivity – workers' ability to accomplish X amount of work in a given period of time.

If you examine major economic transitions throughout history, you can see that productivity improvements drive global economic change. Some of these improvements came about via new technologies, for example shipping advances, railroads, trucks, planes, phones, computers, and the internet. Others derived from advances in work processes, for example assembly lines and business process analysis. In every case, the story is the same: when a technology or practice improves productivity, companies adopt it rapidly.

Recently, market globalization has also contributed significantly to productivity improvements and outsourcing. Market globalization includes:

- Growth of the available global labor market
- Global market growth: access to more consumers in more countries
- Increased connection and cohesion between national markets
- Economic liberalization

- Communications cost reductions
- Improved infrastructure in all countries
- Increased ease of doing business globally
- Convergence (though incomplete) of global business culture
- An increasingly customer-centric focus on quality

Today, we are clearly in the midst of an era of disruptive productivity improvements that are transforming human life on Earth. Consider just a few: solar power, 3D printing, and autonomous (driverless) vehicles, including cars, truck, buses, trains, and drones.

Many organizations, even those that consider themselves highly innovative, are highly resistant to progress and change. New ideas face a tough road to acceptance. Old bureaucratic approaches can become quickly irrelevant or ineffective in a rapidly changing landscape, yet organizations often hold onto those approaches long after they become counterproductive.

"Since 2005, 60% of US job growth has come from independent contractors and freelancers," according to Salim Ismail, founding Executive Director of Singularity University and the author of the best-selling business transformation book, *Exponential Organizations: Why New Organizations are Ten Times Better, Faster, and Cheaper Than Yours (And What To Do About It)*. Salim Ismail describes exponential organizations as "agile, cost-effective, and outsourced."[1]

The expansion of outsourcing is a massive historical and economic trend. The requirements for success are rapidly changing. Outsourcing, as well as other trends such as automation, artificial intelligence, and machine learning, will permeate previously untouched industries and job categories.

You cannot stop outsourcing. However, you can influence the nature of outsourcing. You can plan, guide, and direct outsourcing efforts so that they lead to happier customers, workers, and other stakeholders in every corner of the world. That is what this book is about.

---

[1] https://exponentialorgs.com/

CHAPTER 2

Why Outsource Content Development?

When planned, implemented, and managed well, technical writing outsourcing can result in:

- Improved quality
- Reduced costs
- Expanded capacity at lower cost
- Improved processes
- Cultural advantages
- Improved onshore team morale
- Content development co-located with offshore development teams
- Increased global responsiveness
- Improved writing methodology
- Better productivity per 24-hour period ("Following the Sun")
- Smoother transition to new work models

Improved quality

In any content development operation, excellence is a factor of management. If management is not committed to content quality, then quality is likely to be mediocre or poor. Although offshore content development has a reputation for poor quality, some offshore technical documentation firms are committed to content quality. I know this because I run such a firm.

The process of planning outsourcing, or deciding whether outsourcing is warranted, involves a detailed analysis of business processes to determine which processes or portions of processes can be effectively and cost-effectively outsourced (See Chapter 5, *Assess Process Maturity and Support Structures*). Undertaking this kind of investigation about your organization can uncover process bottlenecks and challenges. You can use the results of the analysis to implement process and quality improvements, whether or not you ultimately pursue outsourcing.

Reduced costs

Outsourcing is primarily driven by a search for lower costs. Over time, those cost savings can be significant (See Chapter 9, *Understand the Economics of Outsourcing*).

Expanded capacity at lower cost

Ideally, outsourcing can give you a larger team, higher output, and lower costs – and this ideal is obtainable.

Improved processes

As noted above, the analysis of business processes that precedes successful outsourcing can lead to significant process improvements. Carefully modifying processes to take advantage of the benefits of outsourcing can result in even greater process improvements.

Cultural advantages

Culture shock is real and poses challenges. People who lack deep exposure to cultures other than their own, or who adopt the attitude that their culture is superior, can cause significant problems in a multicultural workplace. If you are already uncomfortable with or suspicious of *others* it is easy to blame them when something goes wrong. To move past this generally requires team members to:

- Be curious about the other culture.
- Learn about the strengths and weaknesses of the other culture.
- Learn about the strengths and weaknesses of your own culture.
- Learn about yourself. In particular, understand the cultural basis of your own strengths and weaknesses.

When you succeed in overcoming those challenges, you can develop a team of people who understand themselves better, because they have been exposed to people who have a completely different view of the world. A deeper understanding of self can lead to better collaboration and cooperation, a reduction in tension and unresolved conflict in the work environment, and higher productivity.

Improved onshore team morale

Offshore writers typically have fewer years of experience than their onshore counterparts. If offshore writers are given less advanced tasks, onshore writers are able to focus on the more complex tasks that are more interesting to them. They can move from being overworked to having a support staff that assists them. They also have the opportunity to mentor their offshore colleagues. All of this, when properly managed, can result in significantly increased morale for onshore writers. Technical communication professionals with either no outsourcing experience or only negative experiences often find this hard to believe. Nonetheless, I have seen it happen repeatedly.

Sometimes technical writers ask, "Aren't offshore writers bored with low-level work?" In my experience with scores of offshore writers, the answer is no. They are excited to have work that uses their skills, that matters to someone, and that offers a good wage and good benefits. They love learning, including learning how to improve their attention to detail and consistency.

Content development co-located with offshore development teams

Many companies that do not outsource or offshore technical writing maintain significant offshore operations in other domains. Adding technical writers in the same location (or a close time zone) as the engineers, quality assurance staff, product managers, marketers, support staff, or other related teams can yield significant benefits from increased coordination and collaboration.

Increased global responsiveness

If your organization provides products or services in many countries, having a culturally and geographically diverse team can enable you to respond more quickly and with a better cultural understanding of your customers.

Improved writing methodology

One advantage that many offshore writing teams have is a lack of experience with outdated tech writing models. Over the last 20 years, technical writing has been moving from a book model, where you plan, outline, and write manuals or online help systems, to a topic model. In topic-based authoring, you write topics – units of information that can stand alone. Topics are linked to other topics, but they do not depend on the reader having read any other topics previously. Each topic conforms to a type (task, concept, and reference, etc.).

Topic-based authoring enables a great variety of advances in customer experience. Instead of searching for a PDF and then searching within that PDF, users can navigate or search a database of online topics and find the information they need more quickly.[1]

Many offshore writers began by learning to write topic-based content. They have no attachment to the legacy book model and, thus, have no outdated approaches to overcome.

We are now on the cusp of the next transition – to microcontent. For example, the Precision Content methodology[2] enables teams to chunk topics into smaller units, using a *schema* that is based on the latest cognitive science about human learning. This enables automated systems to serve up the exact unit of information that a user seeks. You can type, or speak, your question, and instead of getting a list of 50,000 search results, you get the precise piece of information you are looking for.

---

[1] See *Every Page is Page One: Topic-based Writing for Technical Communication and the Web*, by Mark Baker.

[2] https://www.precisioncontent.com/our-technology/what-is-precision-content/

Better productivity per 24-hour period ("Following the Sun")

If you have two or three teams spread across the globe, one team can be working while another is sleeping. When managed properly, this capability can enable quicker responses and help you get more work accomplished each day. This can be a powerful way to increase your ability to meet project deadlines.

Smoothing transitions to new work models

Any transition takes planning, time, and effort and can be quite difficult. If you have teams of onshore writers that are already fully occupied updating and extending current content, adding transition work that challenges their ways of working can reduce productivity and morale significantly.

Adding an offshore team can help you get over the hump of transition. Because the offshore writers are not wedded to long-established ways of doing things, they can quickly adapt and even help your onshore team to adjust. If the offshore team is already experienced in the new approach, they can be even more effective in smoothing the transition. This can include – but is not limited to – transitions in any of the following areas:

- Content models (topic-based authoring, XML, DITA, etc.)
- Authoring methodologies (e.g., Precision Content method)
- (CCMS) Component Content Management Systems (e.g., Astoria, EasyDITA, Ixiasoft, Vasont, SDL Tridion, and XML Documentation Add-on for Adobe Experience Manager)
- Authoring tools (e.g., Oxygen, XMetaL, Madcap Flare)
- Content quality and terminology management tools (Acrolinx, Hyper-STE)

Management Matters

Effective management is a pre-requisite for effective outsourcing. If your management practices are deficient, outsourcing will likely fail. This part of the book looks at management practices that will make your outsourcing efforts more effective and more likely to succeed. In short, management matters!

CHAPTER 3
Understanding Labor and Management

In thinking about outsourcing, technical communication professionals often conflate two distinct dimensions:

- The location of workers (offshore, onshore, in-house, outsourced)
- The quality of management and of the work experience

It may seem obvious that these two dimensions vary independently. However, people tend to think in generalities. Outsourced, offshore work is assumed to involve bad management and the exploitation of workers. While those things sometimes go together, there is plenty of bad management and exploitation in in-house, onshore work environments as well.

Conditions for workers, and the quality of management, vary greatly. Companies create mini-worlds within themselves. Within these worlds, a lot can go wrong. Good management values workers and treats workers with respect; it also focuses on the factors that increase quality and output and reduce costs. However, often management focuses instead on protecting their turf, personality conflicts, and bigotry, reducing worker morale and organizational effectiveness.

Outsourced content development in particular has a reputation for poor quality, particularly of English content. This reputation is arguably deserved. While it does not apply to every single offshore content development outsourcing firm, many managers have had bad experiences with such firms.

I've had some remarkable encounters with technical communications professionals who seem to firmly believe that their experiences are the only types of outsourcing experiences possible. The idea that outsourcing can actually work well, or that outsourcing will not necessarily reduce quality or lead to layoffs, can inspire reactions of anger and disbelief. And yet, there are all kinds of experiences with outsourcing, just as there are all kinds of experiences with onshore teams. As a technical writer in the US, I personally witnessed both bad and good outsourcing situations.

Again, many of the key success factors for outsourcing are actually key success factors for any kind of business activity. In other words, bad management is the key problem, whether or not outsourcing is involved.

CHAPTER 4

Five Keys to Organizational Success

In almost 40 years of experience in technical documentation and businesses, large and small, I've learned that organizational success depends on the details, and on the corporate culture. How do people interact with each other? What kinds of behavior are encouraged, acceptable, prohibited? How are decisions made?

Like many workers and managers, I've observed a lot of good management and a lot of bad management. I've been thinking for decades about what determines the difference.

I've developed five keys to organizational success. If your organization is going to thrive, these factors are essential, regardless of whether outsourcing is involved.

1. **Values and basic commitments:** Having a strong set of values and basic commitments, and training everyone, at all levels, to live according to those values and basic commitments on a daily, even hourly basis, can avert a tremendous amount of disruption, exploitation, abuse, missed deadlines, bad morale, and low productivity.

2. **Mission and vision:** Having a clear mission and an aspirational vision for the organization, department, or team – and living it every day – enables people to be inspired at work, to truly be themselves, and to exceed their previous limitations.

3. **Accountability for quality:** What makes excellence possible?
   - Having structures in place that hold everyone accountable for quality in everything they do.
   - Discouraging the blame game.
   - Encouraging team members to take personal responsibility for what goes wrong.
   - Teaching principle by example.
   - Not being afraid to say, "I'm sorry. I messed up."

4. **Putting staff first:** As Richard Branson has noted, "The way you treat your employees is the way they will treat your customers."[1] This is also key to overall business success Pay a living wage. Invest heavily in a wide variety of training programs. Ensure that staff are treated fairly and consistently by the organization. Promote a servant-leadership[2] management approach – managers exist to support staff and enable them to succeed, not the other way around. Support managers but be willing to discipline or fire managers who abuse their authority.

5. **Brand promises:** Making clear promises to your customers, and ensuring that those promises are fulfilled every day, makes excellent customer service possible.

How strong is your organization on each of the five factors? When considering an outsourcing partner, it pays to inquire into their strengths and weaknesses in these areas. Often you can learn about these areas by "listening in between the lines."

HIRRAAP

How can you implement these five keys throughout your organization and build a strong culture based on them? The answer comes in the form of an acronym: HIRRAAP (Honesty, Integrity, Rationality, Respect, Access, Awareness, Pay). By focusing on these seven areas, you can dramatically improve organizational effectiveness:

Honesty: Honesty involves a complete refusal to deceive – in other words, never telling lies.

Integrity: Integrity is deeper than honesty. Integrity involves being responsible for your commitments, including your promises – small and large, obvious and implied, as an individual and as an organization.

Rationality: Rationality dictates that logic, not hierarchy, rules, and that reason-based arguments are always welcome.

---

[1] https://www.virgin.com/richard-branson/way-you-treat-your-employees

[2] http://www.servantleaderjournal.com/ten-principles.html

Respect: Respect involves treating every person, including yourself, as a unique individual with enormous, and partly undiscovered, talents and abilities.

Access: Access means that managers and executives are available to staff. Without access, positive change is often impossible.

Awareness: Awareness requires curiosity, humility, and openness. A lack of awareness can lead to denial and dysfunction.

Pay: Pay everyone a living wage. This is a requirement of integrity. Not doing so violates the basic social contract of work.

Honesty

Honesty is telling the truth and not engaging in deception. Of course, being honest does not mean that you tell everything to everyone all the time. Confidentiality is crucial in many business situations, and withholding information is not the same as lying. Lying is knowingly telling a falsehood.

In some Asian cultures, people may lie as a way to avoid challenging authority. For example, a manager gives instructions to a group of workers and asks the group, "Do you understand?" Everyone in the group nods and says, "Yes." Some of the workers may not understand, but rather than say so in front of the group or talk back to the manager, they lie. They may not even think of this as lying.

This kind of behavior can destroy organizations.

Many businesses in the Philippines keep two sets of financial books – one is the truth, and the other is what they show the tax authorities. This is dishonest. It is also illegal and very damaging to the country. People excuse this by saying that the government is corrupt, and the tax money is misspent. But how can the government be expected to behave honestly if the people are dishonest? Likewise, how can employees be expected to behave honestly if management is dishonest?

Of course, some bureaucracies are designed to reinforce and even require participation in corruption. Nonetheless, there is always a role for individual integrity to play. Systems are difficult to improve, but without committed action from honest individuals, systems cannot improve.

In the US, many organizations maintain dishonest management practices. For example, a manager praises one person for work that another person actually accomplished with little participation or support from the person praised. Now, if the manager made a mistake, that may be incompetence, not dishonesty. Honesty does include the factor of intent. But accuracy in business is also crucial.

Or consider a manager who tells a deceptive story to make his group look good. He then requires his staff to tell lies that are consistent with his deception. People often prioritize looking good over the success of a project and over honesty.

If you prioritize anything higher than honesty, you will likely end up lying. The irony is that, by prioritizing something higher than the truth, you will likely damage the very thing you are prioritizing (beginning, perhaps, with your own credibility). Consider a patient who doesn't tell her doctor about all of her symptoms because some of them are embarrassing. In the name of protecting her pride, she could lose her health.

Did you ever hear the saying, "What they don't know won't hurt them?" How do you know? Often it does hurt them. If you're not willing to be responsible for that, don't count on any success in business.

If you really pay attention, you are likely to find yourself lying, or about to lie, many times throughout the day. In each of those moments, you have a choice. Self-awareness is a very good thing. It is essential for personal growth.

Honesty in Outsourcing
When you engage in outsourcing, you are increasing your reliance on trust. Yes, you can implement all kinds of processes to monitor your partner's quality levels and business practices. But ultimately, by sending work outside of your organization – to a different location and perhaps to a different country – you increase risk. That makes it even more crucial that you de-

velop relationships of trust. Dishonesty in outsourcing can be particularly damaging.

Many people in business deny the importance of trust. With regard to their outsourcing partner, they may say, "I don't care how the sausage is made." In other words, they don't care if their partner lies to their staff, mistreats them, underpays them, or undervalues them. If you want to build business processes and teams that can sustain success for many years, such an attitude is short-sighted.

> The role of honesty in outsourcing can be summed up in two words: Everything matters.

Many people do not understand the immense impact of even small lies. Lies destroy trust. Businesses depend on trust to operate. In the absence of trust, no one can count on being treated fairly. This leads to destructive behaviors. People begin asking themselves questions such as the following:

- Why should I be honest with an employer who lies?
- If I cannot count on fair treatment, should I cheat to get ahead?
- Should I take credit for something I didn't do or blame someone else for my mistakes?

Less trust results in more drama, more dysfunction, and less effectiveness. You cannot build a cohesive team that achieves miracles if you sabotage your team with lies.

Lying and Performance Reviews

Many organizations require managers to review staff performance dishonestly. Here's how: organizations often use a common rating scale for evaluations. Managers evaluate employees and determine their ratings in each of several areas, as well as a summary or average rating across areas.

Often the manager will cite examples to explain why an employee got X rating in area A. When these practices are managed effectively and honestly, they can empower individual and organizational performance.

However, some organizations limit the number of high ratings, or require a certain number of low ratings. Upper management or human resources (HR) then requires managers to change the accurate ratings, making them inaccurate. This is dishonest and leads to all kinds of trouble.

Think about some of the effects of this approach. The company has required its managers to lie. Perhaps some honest managers will explain that the accurate rating was X, but they were required to reduce that rating to X-y. This creates a dishonest situation, where decisions about raises and promotions are based on intentionally inaccurate information. Employees feel cheated. Managers feel frustrated, controlled, and forced to operate unethically. Everyone feels devalued, morale plummets, and dysfunction increases.

It would be very easy to eliminate the dishonesty in this system. Rate everyone accurately, but limit the raises. Or change the rating definitions so that more is required to achieve a higher rating. When challenged, executives might offer various rationalizations for their dishonest approach: cost-cutting, avoidance of rating inflation, etc. However, solving these problems doesn't require dishonesty.

To sum up: lying doesn't work. There is always a cost, and often the cost is not revealed until long after the lie is told. When you lie, you may think you fully understand the costs. This is rarely the case.

Integrity

There are many ways to think about integrity, but I want to focus on just a few. For me, integrity has to do with being whole, sound, unimpaired, and undiminished. What does it mean for a person – or an organization – to be this way?

Let's consider integrity as it is expressed in language. Most of language is descriptive. Most technical communication is descriptive. Most conversation is descriptive. Descriptive language is essential to human activity. Some language, however, is generative or creative. This language can constitute action in and of itself – think of requests, promises, and declarations.

For example, when President John F. Kennedy said in 1961 that we would place a man on the moon and return him safely to Earth by the end of the decade, that was a declaration.[3] That declaration did not merely describe reality; it transformed reality. It set in motion a series of events, and it created a powerful set of incentives to which an enormous variety of people responded. Despite Kennedy's assassination two years later, his declaration was fulfilled in 1969.[4]

When you make a declaration, a request, or a promise, you introduce a new intention into the world. You then have the opportunity to live consistently with the new intention you have created – or not. Imagine I promise to meet with you every day this week at 9 am. I then ignore my promise, and when you seek me out every morning, I am unavailable. Because I have not lived up to my promise and have not taken responsibility for my failure to do so, my relationship with you is no longer whole, unimpaired, and undiminished. There is a lack of integrity.

Likewise, if a CEO declares that his company is committed to putting the interests of customers first and then approves a plan to sign up customers for accounts without their knowledge or consent, that CEO is not operating with integrity. He is not living consistently with his declaration.

Operating with integrity does not require that you always keep every promise or succeed in realizing every declaration. Sometimes, circumstances prevent you from doing so. However, operating with integrity requires that you honor your word by living consistently with the commitments you've spoken – even if you never give voice to those commitments and only imply them through your actions.

For example, for years you behave professionally at work. Then, one week, due to some difficult personal challenges, you yell and scream at people in the office, becoming a whirlwind of blame, anger, and viciousness.

You may never have made an explicit promise to behave civilly at work or to treat people well. But you clearly had an implicit commitment to do so.

---

[3] https://youtu.be/TUXuV7XbZvU
[4] https://youtu.be/BD-1iGWZRDA

Operating with integrity in this situation means that you take responsibility for your actions, perhaps by apologizing to those impacted by your erratic behavior and asking them how you can repair the damage.

Rationality

"He just won't listen to reason."

In too many organizations, this statement becomes an expression of resignation. When the boss or a star developer won't listen to reason, it may seem as though there is nothing you can do. The quality of the work, the success of the organization, and the work experiences of the entire staff suffer – everything suffers – because one person feels that he isn't obliged to reason clearly.

> An organization that elevates personality or hierarchy over reason is a danger to itself.

Hierarchy can be a useful and productive mechanism for organizing work. However, taken to the extreme, irrational and destructive actions are often the result.

What does it take to build an organization based on a commitment to rational discourse and decision-making? Ideally this effort starts at the top, with the leaders of the organization encouraging rational discussion and allowing anyone in the organization to challenge the thinking of anyone else, including the CEO.

Unfortunately, many organizations do not benefit from such forward-thinking leadership. It often falls to those lower down the hierarchy to find ways of increasing the role of rational discussion. This requires a great deal of commitment, humility, and creativity.

By focusing clearly on the goal of improving discourse and decisions and avoiding the temptations of power and ego, it is possible to make a difference. Rather than organizing for or against any individual, work with others to expand the space for rational discourse within the organization. Believe in yourself: you have what it takes to turn around a bad situation. (Of course, there are exceptions where very little can be done. In these cases, the best course of action is to leave the organization.)

Transformational Education

Another approach can also yield extraordinary positive results: learning more about yourself through transformational education. It may seem paradoxical, but in a situation where it appears that another person or group is causing huge problems, you can improve matters by learning more about yourself. I have experienced this to be true over and over again. Most people grossly underestimate their abilities, while assuming that they know how to harness all of their potential without support from others.

You can learn a great deal about yourself by reading books, reflecting, meditating, or even exercising. Challenging yourself to accomplish clear goals can provide a valuable education in who you are and what you are really capable of. However, in large groups focused on transformational education, you can often learn things about yourself that will quickly and dramatically improve your performance and effectiveness. This type of education has been essential in enabling me to accomplish something I had no experience with: being a successful entrepreneur and CEO of a fast-growing company.

There are several organizations that offer such education. I recommend Landmark Education,[5] which offers courses in about 100 cities globally.

Respect

Cultures vary widely in the behaviors they consider respectful. For example, in the Philippines, children are taught not to talk back to their parents, their teachers, elder family members, or other authority figures. Respectful behavior means being quiet, doing as you are told, and not challenging authority.

This view of respect may have dramatic consequences. The child listens to the parent, agrees, and does what the parent says, even if the child knows better. As the child becomes an adult, he continues deferring to his elders.

---

[5] http://www.landmarkworldwide.com

His grandfather, whose formative years occurred in a different world, insists on choosing a career for his adult grandchild. The grandchild is considered respectful if he sacrifices his future out of respect for his elder.

Contrast that with respect in a Jewish family in the United States (my childhood background). Civility is important, but so is arguing, challenging, asking questions. A child who is always quiet and never objects to anything would appear disturbed or in some way problematic.

In other words, a Filipino might consider behavior that is respectful in some contexts – my childhood home or, more broadly, the United States – to be disrespectful. To the American, by contrast, the Filipino's behavior might seem subservient.

In an outsourcing situation that includes team members of different cultural backgrounds, it is important to understand what respect means in each culture. Regardless of whether you are at company headquarters or on the periphery, without cultural awareness and a willingness to adjust behaviors that have been a part of your background for longer than you have been alive, you are likely to encounter problems.

For example, in cultures where the word *no* is uttered very infrequently, the word *yes* takes on many meanings. Yes can mean, "Yes, I respect you and I'm trying to listen to what you're saying, but I have no idea what you're talking about." This is just one example of the many types of cross-cultural awareness that can help you succeed. The key is to be interested in learning about each culture, including your own.

Values and Communication

Another way to understand cultural variations in respect is to inquire into each culture's key values. Equality is a key value in the US. If you address an American as sir or ma'am, they may think you are not being professional and lose respect for you. Or they may just be confused and put off, because the experience of being called sir or ma'am is foreign to them. Perhaps they will even think that you are mocking them for acting superior.

By contrast, in many Asian cultures, sir or ma'am are essential when addressing anyone older than you or with greater authority than you.

Every culture has strengths and weaknesses. And inside many strengths are weaknesses and vice versa. Learning to understand another culture can give you insight into the strengths and weaknesses of your own culture. More importantly, cross-cultural understanding can enable you to create a new sense of self that is not limited by your own culture. In order to succeed, you must give up the idea that your culture is superior.

Respect and Expectations

If you tell me you can't do something, I respect that – on one level. But if I respect you, I will have high expectations of you. I may not be willing to accept your "I can't" statement. I may challenge you, based on my appreciation of your capabilities and your potential. This is an essential aspect of effective management.

> In any culture, the most important person to respect is yourself. Do not underestimate yourself. Have high expectations for yourself. Be willing to risk disappointment or failure.

Access

An inaccessible manager can make an employee's job nearly impossible. I don't mean a manager who travels a lot and keeps in touch via email or phone. I mean a manager who almost never meets with staff, virtually or otherwise, and rarely responds to email.

It is remarkable that so many managers and executives fail to appreciate the impact of their lack of availability. If you have no time for someone, you should not be that person's manager.

What can you do when faced with this kind of management? Your options may not be good. You can seek out support from other people. You can collaborate with peers and consult with other managers or executives. You can find a mentor. However, the structure and processes of most companies dictate that, for some things, you need your manager. And if you're out of sync with your manager, you may be working at cross purposes.

In some companies, the human resources department can assist you. Before engaging in an official complaint process, however, explore whether there are less formal avenues to resolve the situation. If not, you may find it necessary to go over your manager's head and contact his boss.

Whatever you do, do not ignore or tolerate such a situation for too long. The repercussions can be quite bad for you and others.

Awareness

Awareness is essential in management. Being aware – especially of the most important aspects of company life – requires curiosity, humility, and openness. "I know everything I need to know" is perhaps the most damaging approach to management.

Whatever else it involves, management is always about people. Be aware of what is going on with people, what is below the surface, and what isn't being said. Are processes working? Are customers happy? What is going on in the organization, with customers, in the industry, and in the world that can affect your operations?

I have found that reading a newspaper is a tremendous aid in maintaining and increasing awareness. There is enormous value in reading a variety of stories daily on a wide range of topics that haven't been pre-selected. If you only consume what you ask for, you miss important events, situations, and trends that may ultimately end up mattering to you a great deal.

Pay everyone a living wage

Why are some workers paid less than it costs them to live? On one level, this occurs because of power imbalances. These workers lack the economic or political power to secure better wages. Wealthier people often complain that low wage earners are a burden on society. If every worker is paid a living wage, however, the burden on society is lightened.

In most cases, a company cannot change society by itself. But companies enjoy wide latitude in how much they pay their employees. Some companies that employ professionals and pay well to attract the best talent still contract out so-called non-essential services to other companies that pay less than a living wage. Why is this acceptable? If it is important to have a clean office, free of bacteria, germs, and infectious disease, why have a cleaning staff that cannot afford proper health care?

In the Philippines, people who work in building security jobs typically work 12 hours per day, 30 days per month. In my view, this should be illegal everywhere. How can such a person maintain a healthy family life, not to mention stay awake and alert for 12 hours every day and be prepared to face danger at a moment's notice?

Are your pay practices based on a sense of entitlement that results in exploitation? Would you be happy with such pay if you had no other job options? How would you feel about your place of work?

Not paying some workers a living wage means that you are not operating with integrity. You are violating the basic social contract of work and failing to keep an implied promise to workers. Morality aside, you're also far more likely to see shoddy work, low morale and productivity, and general dysfunction. You may also encounter protests, strikes, sabotage, and security breaches.

Outsourcing does not reduce or eliminate these issues. Although it may distance you from some of the impact of poor practices, you can't avoid the impact entirely. A vendor who mistreats or underpays its people is likely to have management, execution, and quality problems that will affect the work they do for you.

If you claim to engage in ethical business practices, be consistent with your claim by paying a living wage. Insist that your vendors do so as well or lose your business.

The eleven commandments of ethical business success

1. Always be honest. Always.
2. Respect everyone and everything, in every moment, including yourself.
3. Care about everyone and everything, in every moment.
4. Treat each worker as a gift, king, and miracle.
5. Listen.
6. Identify the problem and the root causes first, before considering solutions.
7. Pay everyone a living wage.
8. Focus on reality, workability, and organizational learning and improvement.
9. Encourage self-expression, full participation, and responsibility for the whole.
10. Reward cooperation and discourage vicious, disrespectful competition.
11. Include your corporate values in evaluations and hiring decisions.

I have built a successful outsourcing business based on these principles, developed over decades of work experience in the United States and almost another decade in the Philippines. It is not an open question whether a business can succeed using these principles; my business has, and I have every reason to believe that other businesses can as well.

The myth of business necessity

Many people believe that being successful in business requires them to leave their ethics at the door. In their personal lives they may believe in treating others as they wish to be treated, but in business they think that success requires them to abandon this idea.

There are three fundamental problems with this view:

Where is the evidence?

If you have not consistently applied a high ethical standard to business, over many years, how do you know that it cannot work? Just trying doesn't count. It takes persistence to succeed, in ethics and everywhere else.

Ethical behavior supports success

The secret of ethics is that ethical behavior supports success. Consistently respecting others and treating them well opens doors that ethically compromised individuals cannot access. And in cultures where every individual is supported and given the chance to thrive, organizations can achieve miracles.

Success isn't worth your soul

Is success really more important to you than doing the right thing? Too often, this question goes unasked. Will business success really lead to a better life if it comes at the cost of your soul?

For me, the answer is no. Even if it turned out that bad behavior paid off more in narrow financial terms, I have no interest in being involved in such a business. It is enough for me that I can succeed while maintaining my ethical standards. That is what I want to do. I don't care to be successful at the expense of others. Do you?

Your Roadmap to Outsourcing Success

What are the steps involved in successful outsourcing? This part presents a basic roadmap. Each chapter in this part covers one segment of the roadmap. Some activities overlap with others, and you don't necessarily need to perform them in the order listed. I suggest that you read through these chapters, then decide how to proceed based on your priorities. Also, be sure to involve technical communications professionals in your planning. They will provide essential understanding of the content development process.

Here is the basic sequence of the roadmap:

- Assess process maturity and content development support structures
- Create a vision and goals
- Find allies in your organization
- Understand issues, fears, pitfalls, and risks
- Understand the economics of outsourcing
- Choose an outsourcing scenario and location
- Choose an outsourcing partner
- Create a plan
- Sell your plan to upper management
- Sell your plan to your team and colleagues
- Stage a pilot/test-drive
- Get started: kick-off, training, travel
- Set up structures for ongoing success

CHAPTER 5
Assess Process Maturity and Support Structures

Two fundamental mistakes can doom outsourcing efforts:

1. Adding outsourcing to an unsustainable set of processes
2. Providing less support to outsourced resources than to in-house resources

To avoid these mistakes, start by considering how your work gets accomplished now. In particular, consider several key dimensions:

- **Communication structures:** Bug or ticket tracking system, code repository, component content management system/documentation repository, intranets/wikis, chat groups, meetings, project document repositories, etc.

- **Types of project work:** Initial estimates/scoping, project planning, site/folder/app preparation and updates, issue resolution, research, writing, reviews, testing, graphics work, integration of graphics, preparation for translation, localization quality control, etc.

- **Roles:** Who does what on the team? What support do they have and from whom? Include all the related teams that the content developers interact with.

- **Processes:** How do technical writers gather information? Do they use product prototypes, project documents (requirements documents, design documents, functional specifications, user interface specifications, test plans), or bug reports? Do they rely on direct contact with QA, engineering, marketing, project management, or support personnel? How frequently are prototypes, project documents, and bug reports updated? How accessible are personnel on related teams? Are documentation reviews performed? Do the other team members provide detailed feedback? What kinds of issues occur with these processes?

Process maturity

Next, perform an initial assessment of your current process maturity. How capable are your processes of sustainably supporting the work of the organization? I recommend starting with the original Capability Maturity Model, which was developed by Watts Humphrey, first at IBM and later at the Software Engineering Institute (SEI) at Carnegie Mellon University.[1] Several technical communicators and content strategists have expanded that model to better match their specialties, including JoAnn Hackos, Rahel Anne Bailie, Kathy Wagner, and Sarah O'Keefe.[2]

Nothing can completely substitute for an in-depth evaluation of your organization's process maturity, however, you can perform an informal initial assessment using the descriptions of each level below: Initial, Repeatable, Defined, Managed (Capable), or Optimizing (Efficient).[3]

- **Level 1 – Initial:** At this level, processes are reactive and unpredictable. Process control or measurement is absent. Discussions about process improvement are difficult. For example, you may have written specifications, but they are not kept up to date. A bug tracking system may exist, but technical writers cannot access it. Developers are too busy to provide feedback on documentation. QA personnel do not test – and rarely review – documentation. Technical writers struggle to learn about user interface changes.

- **Level 2 – Repeatable:** At this level, processes are documented at the functional team level, but they may still be largely reactive. Dependencies between functional teams are handled on an ad-hoc basis; for example, prototypes and specifications may be regularly updated, but not regularly shared with other teams. The product development lifecycle may be documented, but it is not strictly followed by all teams. Frequent breakdowns and conflicts require resolution by team managers or upper management.

---

[1] You can find resources at the CMMI Institute (https://cmmiinstitute.com/).

[2] Larry Kunz has written an article that provides a high-level survey of these models: https://larrykunz.wordpress.com/2015/02/06/your-guide-to-content-strategy-maturity-models/.

[3] These descriptions differ from the CMMI model to focus on content development issues.

- **Level 3 – Defined:** At this level, processes are clearly characterized, documented, and understood by all participants. Processes are primarily pro-active. All functional teams are aligned on almost all processes. Procedures, tools, and standards are defined at the organizational level. Dependencies between teams are well understood, incorporated into processes, and supported by all participants. For example, technical writers start receiving project documents early in the product development process, are included in project meetings, and have access to relevant databases and other information sources. Established processes for informing technical writers of user interface changes usually work well. All functional teams provide documentation feedback. The documentation team is likely to use topic-based authoring.

- **Level 4 – Managed (Capable):** At this level, processes are quantitatively managed. Each participant, or at a minimum each functional team, has interim production targets that support organizational targets. Functional teams, including documentation teams, have input into user interface design or product design. Some customer feedback is incorporated into product development. Technical writers can rely on both the processes and personnel of other teams to support their efforts. Deadlines – team, organization, interim, and final – are usually met. Due to a solid foundation of mature processes that support effective collaboration, both functional teams and the organization as a whole can use quantitative measurements to improve productivity, quality, and delivery. Technical writers are more likely to implement advanced technologies to improve the user experience and incorporate user participation in their work.

- **Level 5 – Optimizing (Efficient):** At this level, processes are continually tweaked and improved. Innovation at every level is encouraged and incorporated. The organization – as well as some teams and individual employees – are thought leaders within the industry.

Using these descriptions, determine your organization's process maturity level. While your rating should include the impact of various teams and how they collaborate with each other, you can focus on the technical content development aspects. Your rating may not be valid as an assessment of the overall product development process maturity. Your concern is to accurately assess the processes that directly affect your team's output. Consider each activity that your team is involved in. What works or doesn't work about that activity?

Translating the numbers

What do these levels mean for your organization?

- **Process maturity below 2:** If your process maturity level is below 2, I don't recommend outsourcing in the near term. At this level, outsourcing can place greater strain on already-deficient processes through increased geographical dispersion, cultural and language differences, differing professional backgrounds and experience levels, and increased training and management requirements. Stakeholders may also blame outsourcing for disappointing outcomes, reducing the likelihood that your organization will take advantage of outsourcing in the future. Before you prepare to outsource, your organization needs to make significant process improvements.

- **Process maturity above 2 but less than 3:** If your process maturity level is between 2.0 and 2.9, I recommend improving your processes to level 3 before – or alongside – any outsourcing initiative. At these levels, process improvements are often relatively straightforward. That said, support from upper management and broad organizational alignment are crucial for success. As long as process deficiencies are well understood, and you have alignment on improving processes as part of the outsourcing rollout, you can achieve long-term success. In fact, the effort to plan outsourcing often produces fruitful ideas about organizational process improvements.

- **Process maturity 3 or greater:** If your process maturity level is 3.0 or greater, your organization is ready to outsource.

CHAPTER 6
Create a Vision and Goals

What matters to you about your content development? Quality? Efficiency? Process integrity? Accuracy? Volume produced per week or month? Creating a vision for your content development and setting goals can keep you on track.

Envision success

What does technical writing team success look like to you? Creating a specific vision, including a complete mental image, recorded details, and visual media, can enable you and your team to align as creative, collaborative partners. You can perform this exercise yourself at first then later repeat it with your team.

- First, write down, in detail, your vision of a perfect content development scenario. Include all the elements that matter to you. Consider the requirements of your organization, but don't allow the past to completely define your vision. Include outsourcing if that is part of your ideal or your requirements.
- Second, draw your vision. You can use any medium you like. Even if you do not consider yourself to be artistic, this part of the exercise may help you notice important dimensions and details that matter to you.

A vision addresses the gap between what is real now and what you aim to create. If you resist aspects of reality that you don't like, you cause their persistence. However, if you accept reality as it is, and create a vision for how it can be in the future, you can create a new reality.

When creating your vision, don't sell yourself short. Don't limit yourself to what has been done before in your organization. One important aspect to consider is user input, or some form of user participation. Do you know anything about how your users consume your content and how helpful they find that content?

Years ago it was nearly unheard of for technical writers to survey users, or gain any access or information regarding users and how they interact with technical content. Today, product development trends such as Agile, Scrum, and Lean Development emphasize user participation in product development. In some organizations, intelligent content provides technical writers data on which topics users access and how long they spend on each page. This can be quite helpful. For example, if users keep switching pages every few seconds, they may be having difficulty finding exactly the information they need.

You may think, "I know what matters to me. Why do I need to write it down or discuss it? It's clear."

Well, maybe. But I have repeatedly found that:

- Writing down, drawing, or creating a vision in some concrete medium is incredibly empowering and revealing. Why? Because a vision is, by definition, not reality. You cannot look around and be reminded of your vision, unless you design your environment to remind you.
- Creating and discussing a vision with others, when done in an authentic, curious, and inspired manner, consistently produces greater clarity and power than creating a vision alone. It helps if the participants in the discussion all care about the issues – and about each other.

Once you've created a vision with your writing team, consider going through this exercise with other stakeholders. People are much more willing to own something that they had a hand in creating.

This phase is less important if you have mature processes in place (level 3 or above as described in Chapter 5, *Assess Process Maturity and Support Structures*). For example, if your organization has been successful in implementing and following Agile development processes, you can create a plan to fully include the offshore team in those processes. You may not need a clear vision and goals for the transition, because the expanded team will fold into your existing structure.

To enhance your vision, consider as many dimensions as you can. Be sure to consider all phases of change: planning, transition, start-up, and ongoing implementation. Consider dimensions such as:

- How will writers work? Where will they be located? How will they communicate and cooperate with other writers, other functional teams, customers, etc.?
- Who will participate in designing the new processes? How will people be oriented to new ways of working?
- What types of training will be provided? To whom, where, how, and how frequently?
- How will management operate? Where will managers be located? How will they communicate and cooperate?
- How will managers at different levels interact? What is the role of upper management?
- How will processes be documented, monitored, and managed?
- How will quality, results, and costs be measured? How will goals be set and achieved?
- How will projects be reviewed? How will a culture of continuous improvement become institutionalized?
- What opportunities for growth and development will be available to personnel in each location?
- How will work relationships be established and deepened? Will travel be involved? Who will travel, and how often?
- What will the work environment be like? Will people enjoy their work? How will workers be supported? What team-building programs or activities will be available?

Implement your vision

Now that you have a vision, display it prominently. Then, consider what it will take to close the gap between your vision and your current reality. In creating goals, do not limit yourself to the factors already measured by your organization; instead, integrate all dimensions of your vision.

For example, you might aim for the following goals:

- Within three months, documentation review meetings will occur twice per release for each topic set, with participation from all functional teams.
- The QA team will test all documented procedures for all releases.
- Within six months of starting outsourcing, the quality of all content will surpass current measures.
- All simple questions from the outsourced team will be responded to within 12 hours, and answered within 24 hours. For larger questions and requests, a plan will be agreed upon within 48 hours.
- Within six months, each new writer will be able to support two different feature teams.
- Outsourcing will expand team capacity at 15% lower cost than local expansion over the first two years.

CHAPTER 7
Find Allies in Your Organization

To succeed in either process change or outsourcing, you need alignment from partners in different functional teams. Ideally you can start with upper management; in fact, the initial request to explore outsourcing often originates there. That said, upper management may not fully appreciate all of the requirements and costs that a successful outsourcing effort entails. If that's the case, you need to invest the time and effort to create comprehensive alignment on your vision and goals as well as on the planning, transition, and startup phases that are crucial to success.

Start with your supporters and mentors, or with the most open-minded and thoughtful people in the organization. Share your vision and invite others to contribute to it. Be willing to start over in creating the vision with each person or group. You can still advocate for your priorities, but you need to fully include all stakeholders in the process.

In addition, the strategies outlined in Chapter 13, *Sell Your Plan: Selling Up*, and Chapter 14, *Sell Your Plan: Selling Down*, can help you gain allies.

CHAPTER 8
Understand Issues, Fears, Pitfalls, and Risks

When outsourcing goes wrong, it typically is due to one of the following issues:

- **Location:** Clearly, dispersing work across the globe can lead to problems. Often, however, problems have more to do with some of the other issues listed here.

- **Function:** Different kinds of professionals often don't communicate well with each other – or even understand each others' roles. For example, have your offshore product engineers worked with technical writers before?

- **Inclusion:** Onshore, in-office personnel benefit tremendously from their proximity and accessibility to each other. Specific plans, structures, and processes must be implemented to replace the benefits of proximity in a distributed work environment. At a minimum, offshore writers need all of the training, access, communication channels, and support that in-house writers enjoy.

- **Language:** Language issues can be formidable. For non-native English speakers, it can be difficult to overcome grammar and writing blind spots. Editing and quality control are essential, as are careful hiring processes and ongoing training.

- **Experience level:** Often outsourcing is blamed for dramatically lower productivity among the offshore writers, when in fact the difference is primarily due to experience. A writer with twenty-five years' experience can work much better and faster than a writer with two years' experience, regardless of location or other factors.

- **Competence:** In every country, competence varies. If offshore hiring practices are deficient, an entire offshore team may lack the ability to learn and improve enough to succeed. That does not mean that outsourcing itself doesn't work.

- **Culture:** Cultural awareness is crucial. It is often difficult to distinguish cultural issues from language issues. If writers are not asking questions, it may be because asking questions is not encouraged in their culture, and their management has not provided the transformational education required to move beyond their cultural limitations. Having a mix of cultures and language backgrounds in each location can be immensely helpful. Even one person in each location of a different culture can make a huge difference.

- **Management:** Most outsourcing failures can be traced to poor management, because management by definition is responsible for overall success. Humility and curiosity can help a great deal. Seek out mentors who have experienced similar situations. Believe in yourself, and don't give up. Persistence is invaluable. Be sure to provide for the following in all locations:
  - Effective change management
  - Adequate training and support
  - Cross-cultural learning, relationship development, and management training

One of the challenges of outsourcing is the one-dimensional views that many people have about it. Some outsourcing myths are based in actual experience or real situations, but they become generalized far beyond their true range.

Here are some guidelines to avoid the worst pitfalls:

- Include technical communications professionals in outsourcing decisions; otherwise quality will suffer. (Not doing this can also lead to layoffs that must later be reversed.)
- Employ experienced editors; otherwise the quality of content from offshore writers will not meet the highest standards.
- Include offshore writers in wikis, meetings/calls, emails, chats, etc.
- Insure adequate budget for training, travel, management, and IT support.
- Employ creative, resourceful leadership in each location.

CHAPTER 9
Understand the Economics of Outsourcing

How much can you save by outsourcing content development? This question can be tricky. Even if your outsourcing goals are much broader than cost savings, the way you approach this question can influence your success.

A common mistake is to compare the cost of labor between two countries and conclude that the difference in labor costs is approximately equal to the cost savings from outsourcing. In fact, the cost savings from outsourcing are always less than the labor cost differential and usually much less.

For example, the hourly cost charged by an offshore vendor may be as low as 20–35% of the salaries paid in your location. That does not mean you can save 65–80%. There are significant additional costs required to make outsourcing work. These include travel, training, and management costs. Each of these costs involves hours or days spent by specific people, all of whom are paid in one way or another by your company.

In addition to increased training, the productivity of the outsourced staff may be lower than your current staff. This is often due in large part to lower experience levels at the offshore location. It also can result from cultural differences – both national and corporate. If it takes two offshore writers to do the work of one current writer, your savings percentage will be significantly reduced. There will also be significantly higher startup costs in the first year of a long-term engagement.

In an in-house, offshore situation, where your company already has significant sunk costs in an offshore office location and staff, there may be a difference of up to 90% between offshore pay levels and pay in your organization's home country. In this situation, your company is already paying some of the additional costs that outsourcing requires.

If you can save 10–25% over a period of several years, that is a big success. Higher savings may be possible for in-house situations, but that is partly due to the sunk costs and ongoing expenses that are usually excluded from these calculations. Savings of 60% or higher are rarely possible. Anyone who expects such savings is not considering all of the relevant factors.

How should you deal with a manager who claims 85% cost savings? Regardless of your status in the organization or your relationship with that manager, if you care about your organization, you must find a way to educate them or challenge their assumptions. Use your best diplomatic skills.

Setting your organization up for success

Outsourcing can fail if your organization refuses to make the necessary investments in its success. For example:

- Demanding the same level of productivity from offshore writers with 1–4 years of experience as onshore writers with 20 years of experience.
- Allocating zero budget for managing offshore writers. You need effective management, both offshore and onshore.
- Allocating zero budget for travel and training.
- Allocating zero budget for editing and quality control.

Many executives who are perfectly aware of the need to provide resources and support for onshore personnel, assume that such expenses aren't necessary for offshore workers. In reality, to ensure outsourcing success, you usually need extra funding for training, travel, editing, and management. Often, you need a larger ratio of writers to content and extra time to develop group cohesion and collaboration across continents or countries.

Understanding cost changes: an example

Let's examine the possible cost changes for a software development organization that includes a team of experienced technical writers in an expensive labor market in the United States. The key parameters for this example are:

- The technical writers on the existing team have an average of 15 years of experience. There is a cap on full-time employees; no more can be added. Local contract writers, whose pay is roughly equal to the pay and benefits of the full-time employees, cost at least $100 per hour.

- Due to their experience, the writers conduct peer editing. Therefore, the existing writing team does not have editors or other quality control personnel. Each writer has many years of in-depth product knowledge.

- The writers have developed excellent working relationships with staff across other functional teams.

- Process maturity is high – at least 3.0 – across the entire organization. (See Chapter 5, *Assess Process Maturity and Support Structures*.)

The company is adding two new products, which means this team's work is expected to double in the next six months. Eight offshore, outsourced writers will be added to the existing team of four writers. Because the offshore writers are both less experienced and new to the products, the initial expectation is that it will take two offshore writers to do the work of one onshore writer. The goal is to reduce that ratio to 1.5:1 within six months. The offshore writers will also require editing and quality control.

Table 9.1 shows the hourly cost for offshore staff, including writers, editors, QA, and a team lead.

Table 9.1 – Offshore writing team hourly cost summary

Team Member	Hourly Cost
8 writers ($25/hour each)	$200
1 quality control specialist	$30
1 senior editor	$60
1 team lead	$40
Total team cost (11 people)	**$330**

Dividing the total team cost ($330/hour) by the number of writers (8), the hourly cost per writer is $41.25.

Initially, two writers are required to match the output of one onshore writer, so the cost comparison is $82.50/hour vs. $100/hour for the onshore writer. That cost is expected to diminish to $61.88 after 6 months.

However, there are additional costs that need to be included. These are summarized in Table 9.2 and described below.

Table 9.2 – Additional costs

Description	Cost
Initial travel and training	
Training planning and development ($100 × 40 hours)	$4,000
2 weeks of the manager's labor ($150 × 80 hours)	$12,000
Airfare, lodging, local transport, food, etc.	$5,000
2 weeks of the offshore team's time ($330 × 80 hours)	$26,400
Initial travel and training total	**$47,400**
Offshore team ramp up ($330 × 40 hrs)	**$13,200**
Initial support costs ($100 × 40 hrs)	**$4,000**
Training and support ($100 × 10/wk × 26 wks)	**$26,000**

- **Initial travel and training:** This includes travel and living expenses for the onshore manager to go to the offshore location for 2 weeks to train the team. It also includes planning and developing the training, 2 weeks of the manager's labor, airfare and living expenses, and 2 weeks of the offshore team's time. Total: $47,400

- **Offshore team ramp-up:** For the first 2 weeks after training, a variety of issues (learning, technical, and logistical) will likely limit the offshore team's productivity to about half its normal rate. This adds one week of additional cost. Total: $13,200

- **Initial support costs:** Support from both IT and writing staff will be needed to get the offshore team up and running. Total: $4,000

■ **Ongoing training and support:** The onshore writing team will need to spend time training and assisting the offshore writers, particularly in the first six months. Total: $26,000

Using these figures, let's calculate the costs for the first and second six-month periods and compare those costs to the cost of adding the equivalent number of onshore writers. Table 9.3 compares these costs.

Table 9.3 – First and second six-month periods compared

Description	1st 6 mos	2nd 6 mos
Offshore labor ($330 × 40 hrs × 26 wks)	$343,200	$343,200
Additional initial costs	$64,600	N/A
Additional ongoing costs (2nd 6 mos @ 75%)	$26,000	$19,500
Total cost per 6-month period	$433,800	$362,700
Hourly cost for 8 offshore writers	$52.14[a]	$43.60[b]
Hourly cost to match onshore productivity (1st 6 mos: offshore × 2. 2nd 6 mos: × 1.5)	$104.28	$65.40
Hourly cost vs. onshore writers @ $100/hr	+$4.28	-$34.60
Total cost vs. onshore writers (rounded)	+$17,805	-$215,904
Total first year savings (rounded)	$198,099	
Percentage savings in the first year	19%	
Percentage savings in the second year	42%	

[a] ($433,800/26 weeks/40 hours per week/8 writers)

[b] ($362,700/26 weeks/40 hours per week/8 writers)

This is a simplified example that does not take into account holidays, vacations, additional travel or training, technical or logistical issues, process changes, or quality problems. And, crucially, this assumes mature processes and good management in both locations.

Note the huge difference between the first-year and second-year savings. In both cases, of course, your actual savings may vary widely from the example. However, examining the example you can see why claims of, say, 85% cost savings are generally not credible.

CHAPTER 10

Choose an Outsourcing Scenario

There are many ways to outsource. That said, the least expensive options will almost always be offshore.

Locations

An *onshore* work location is in the same country or region as your offices in a wealthy country (e.g., the US, the UK, or New Zealand). If your offices are in Vancouver, Canada, then Toronto, Canada, would be an onshore location. Onshore has cultural and language advantages, may have proximity and time zone advantages, and is typically the highest-cost option.

A *nearshore* work location is typically in the same time zone or a close time zone, in a low- or medium-cost country. For example, if your offices are in London, then Prague would be a nearshore location. With nearshore locations, cultural and language barriers may be an issue. Distance may or may not be an issue. Costs are generally less than onshore and more than offshore.

An *offshore* work location is in a lower-cost country, usually with a large time zone difference. For example, if your offices are in Austin, Texas, then Manila, Philippines, would be an offshore location. Offshore work has cost advantages, and the wide time zone difference can enable more work to be accomplished in each 24-hour period. There may be cultural and language barriers, as well as distance and time-zone difficulties.

A co-located work location places technical writers in the same time zone or location as engineers, product developers, testers, or other relevant teams. For example, if your main technical writing team, product management, and marketing staff are located in Denver, Colorado, and most of your engineers and product testers are in Bengalaru, India, then Pune, India, would be a co-location.

Service providers

In-house situations do not involve service providers. Instead, your company directly employs either existing or new staff. In-house/offshore can work quite well if your company already has operations offshore and the ability to hire and manage the needed personnel there. The costs of starting up offshore operations can be very high.

Outsourced situations involve external vendors who provide services to your company. Consider three types of service providers:

- **Writing firms:** These companies specialize in content development. They have experience in hiring and managing writers, and often related personnel such as graphic artists. They can typically create content for a wide variety of industries. Their staff may be familiar with the latest technical writing methodologies and tools.

- **Specialist firms:** These companies employ experts in specific fields, sometimes at the PhD level. These experts are often very good writers. They are generally limited to their specialty, have very high costs, and may not be familiar with the latest technical writing methodologies and tools.

- **Generalist firms:** These companies employ a wide variety of professionals. They often focus on fields such as software development or other IT work. They typically have experience with large projects, and large staffs that enable them to scale projects up quickly. However, they may not have experience hiring and managing writers, nor are they likely to have competencies in the latest technical writing methodologies and tools.

CHAPTER 11
Choose an Outsourcing Partner

How do you select an outsourcing vendor? Ultimately, you want to develop a solid relationship with a partner you can trust. You also want a vendor who has the capabilities to meet your needs and a broad commitment to excellence. After all, the goal is to make your life easier, not harder.

This is a tall order, but have faith that you can find the right vendor for you. Here are some steps that will help:

1. **Be careful about the country you choose:** Consider factors such as language, infrastructure, economic growth, stability, and cultural fit. If you need content written in English, for example, consider the prevalence and status of English in that country.

2. **Get to know your vendor:** Have several conversations – ideally in person, but if not, via video or at least voice. Do you feel comfortable with the people you talked to? Can you clearly understand each other? Do they seem knowledgeable, competent, and honest? What seems to be most important to them? Do you think they share your values, or have similar values and business approaches?[1]

3. **Learn about your vendor's approach to management:** You don't need to share your own management philosophy. Instead, ask revealing questions. You can incorporate these questions in your vendor application or include them in conversation. For example:

   - What are your quality control processes? Please explain in detail.

   - Explain your quality story – how do you create and ensure content quality? Ask for this explanation in writing, so you can assess the quality of the writing.

---

[1] Of course, you need to provide leeway for cultural differences. And you need to be careful about a) making excuses for people based on a limited understanding of their culture, or b) assuming that you understand what someone means (or that they understand what you mean) if you are not experienced in communicating with people from that culture.

- Describe your staff training programs. What types of training do you provide? What percentage of your total payroll is spent on training and staff development?

- One of your employees unexpectedly missed two days of work due to a miscarriage. She communicated that she had a medical emergency. How do you handle this when she returns to work?

- What benefits do you offer your staff? What qualifications, requirements, and limitations apply to each benefit?

- Has each staff member of your staff signed a confidentiality agreement? What other policies do you have in place to protect client data?

- How many resignations have you had per year per 100 staff?

- How often does each employee get to meet one-on-one with someone in management?

- Do people in your organization, including your managers, listen to each other? Can you cite examples?

- How does the salary of your lowest-paid employee compare to the local minimum wage? To the local cost of living?

Find a way to independently investigate how the vendor's employees feel about their jobs. Perhaps someone on your staff or in their networks lives in the vicinity of the vendor's place of business, and can casually talk to employees. Perhaps online searches will yield interesting information. You don't want to entrust your content to employees who are unhappy with their company or their jobs.

4. **Take IT and data security very seriously:** Obviously, you'll want your vendor to sign a non-disclosure agreement (NDA) or a contract with a confidentiality clause. Ensure that their employee and consultant contracts include confidentiality clauses as well.

   In addition, consider the networks you might share. How will your vendor ensure that your online resources and data are completely secure? If necessary, what protocols might you establish together?

Ask about your vendor's security policies. For example, your vendor should probably ban the use of USB devices, and employees' mobile phones should never be plugged into vendor-owned computers.

If your company has an outsourcing or vendor management department, they will likely have standard security practices for you to follow in working with vendors. If not, consult with your security, finance, or IT departments. You may need to facilitate communication between the vendor's IT staff and the appropriate parties in your company.

5. **Understand the vendor's ownership and organizational structure:** What is the primary work of the company? Is the company owned or run by someone with technical communication or content experience? What is the history of the company? Who are their customers? You can often find some of this information on the company's site; you can find additional information by looking up the company's leaders on Linkedin.

6. **Ask for references or find them on your own:** Search for testimonials, reviews, critiques. By doing thorough research, you may be able to avoid a world of headaches and wasted expenditures.

7. **Be very careful about contracts:** Aim for simplicity. Make sure you understand. Of course, you'll want any contract between your company and a vendor to be reviewed by your legal department, outsourcing or procurement department, or outside legal counsel. However, do not rely on those parties alone. Make sure that you understand everything in the contract. How will conflicts be dealt with? Will the laws of your country, state, or local jurisdiction apply or those of the vendor? What are the agreements about payment? What happens in case of non-performance? See Appendix A for a sample contract.

You may be tempted to create a long vendor application and make the vendors do all the work. This can be helpful, to an extent. However, no questionnaire can replace what you will learn by speaking individually with each vendor. Doing independent research will also give you confidence and enable you to cross-check the vendor's claims. You can then request explanations for any apparent contradictions.

CHAPTER 12

Create a Plan

After you have alignment on a clear vision, it's time to discuss goals and your plans for achieving them. This plan should include start-up phase activities (See Chapter 16, *Get Started: Kick-off, Training, and Travel*).

You need to think through all aspects of the transition and your new modes of operation. Here are three important elements for your plan:

- **Process definition:** How will the new content development process work? Who will play which role? How many levels of review will there be, and which kinds? Who will perform each review? How will technical questions get answered? Project questions? Business questions? How will you include your offshore team in the process?
- **Estimates:** Will your team produce project estimates or proposals? If so, how? What skills and experience will they draw on? What resources will they use? How long will it take them? What meetings will be involved? Think about how this will happen in the new configuration.
- **Measurements:** How will you measure success? What targets will be included in your vendor agreement? How will progress reports work?

You can use the checklist in Table 12.1 to help create your plan. You may not need a section for each item in the checklist, and you can vary the order in which you address each item. Some items may not be in question, and can be omitted or mentioned briefly.

Your plan will be useful during all phases. In two years, for example, you can compare your results to the vision, goals, and details described in your original plan.

Table 12.1 – Outsourcing plan checklist

Issue or area to include	Included?
Process maturity, support structures, team description, productivity vs. workload, types of content, tasks	
Current issues and challenges	
Vision for improved capacity, effectiveness, quality, etc.	
Goals	
Key stakeholders	
Proposed outsourcing scenario, vendor(s), offshore team size and description	
Vendor pilot or evaluation plan	
Transition plan: kick-off, travel, training, ramp-up	
Ongoing training, travel, and support structures	
Cost analysis	
Process change details: content review, issue resolution, question answering, project estimation, quality measurement, information sharing, team communications, cross-functional communications, etc.	
Reporting, monitoring, evaluation, and management processes	
Editing and quality control staffing and processes	
Management staffing and processes	
Key success factors	
Potential issues, pitfalls, and risks	

Issue or area to include	Included?
Expected results vs. goals	
Proposed implementation timeline	
Questions to consider; additional information to gather	

Putting your plan together: a sample

As a technical communications professional, you will no doubt have your own ideas on how to most effectively structure your plan for your audience. For example, you may want to include charts, graphs, diagrams, pictures, sample documents, or tracking spreadsheets. The sample plan provided here is meant to give you ideas. Reading it should provide detailed guidance on the factors to consider for each stage of implementation.

Technical writing outsourcing plan

Introduction: *[Summarize the impetus/need for the plan, the purpose of the plan, and perhaps general conclusions and areas of inquiry. The introduction can also contain a problem statement.]*

In April, 2017, it became clear that the current resources of the PRODUCT technical writing team were inadequate to the expected workload, and that this was likely not a temporary situation. With the support of EXEC1 and EXEC2, as well as MANAGER1, exploration of potential solutions began. Research and discussion suggested that carefully selecting an offshore outsourcing partner and implementing a strategy of partial outsourcing could, if managed effectively, yield a cost-effective solution, without reducing quality or other service metrics.

Due to the risks of such a change in business operations, careful planning was seen as essential. The purpose of this plan is to fully explain the current situation, propose a plan for change, and fully explain the potential benefits and risks of the plan, noting the key success factors, key budgetary considerations, and schedule dependencies.

Key Stakeholders: *[List stakeholders]*

Section 1 – The Current Situation: *[Outline the current situation.]*

Currently, the PRODUCT technical writing team consists of six experienced technical writers, plus one documentation manager. The range of technical writing experience is from 10 years to 27 years. The average experience level of the writers is 15.5 years. Their average time at the company is 11 years, and their average time on the product is 7.6 years. The manager has been on the product for 10.5 years.

The productivity of the team has increased continually. The product features supported have grown, and the content delivered has doubled in the last 2 years. Further growth, which is expected, will require a larger team. Efficiencies have already been achieved via various methods short of team growth.

Both the larger PRODUCT team and the technical writing team benefit from mature processes (currently rated between levels 3 and 4 of the Capability Maturity Model). While the technical writing team benefits from mostly mature processes, they also take advantage of proximity with other parts of the PRODUCT team, working in the same office. Most writers work from home 1-2 days per week, and one writer works remotely most of the time.

The writers use prototypes that are updated and maintained by the QA team specifically for them. They access the bug database and code repository. They participate in feature team meetings and other product meetings. Currently each writers supports between 2 and 4 feature teams.

Currently there is a long list of documentation improvements on hold. These include creating a more advanced customer portal that would enable the team to track customer documentation access and enable customers to participate actively in the documentation update process. While the support team can perform most of the design and implementation, the system rollout will require the creation of significant new content.

Section 2 – Vision: *[Outline your vision of the future.]*

Discussions with a wide variety of stakeholders yielded the following components of an ideal future state:

- Documentation quality continuously improves by at least 5% per month.
- Technical writing capacity is sufficient to support product growth and to enable the technical writing team to continually break new ground in serving customers.
- The technical writing team has the time to participate in feature meetings starting in the requirements stage. This will increase writer product knowledge and team cohesion and enable writers to provide more input into product and user interface design.
- The writing team is expanded with the addition of an outsourced, offshore team. A large time-zone difference will enable the offshore writers to work while the onshore team sleeps, yielding more results per 24-hour period.

Section 3 – Goals: *[Objectives for the project.]*

The following goals were agreed upon in the PRODUCT team meeting on DATE:

- Each writer participates on no more than two feature teams, enabling writers to stay abreast of requirements, plans, and designs.
- The offshore writing team will be fully included in all repositories, wikis, and communication channels. Most meetings will be recorded, and some meetings will be scheduled to accommodate both teams.
- After the first year, quality measures for the offshore team will equal or exceed the measures of the onshore team at the start of the project. (We assume that both teams will continuously improve.)
- After the first year, the productivity of the offshore writers will be at least 60% of the onshore writers.
- For the second year, the cost of the offshore team will be at least 20% less than additional onshore writers who produce the same amount of content would cost.

Section 4 – Competitive Pilot: *[Plans for a pilot]*

We have agreed to stage a competitive pilot project, involving at least three offshore vendors. Each of the vendors will receive the same initial description of the pilot. If they accept the terms they will receive the same source information. They will be granted access to technical writers and other personnel as needed to answer questions. The duration of the pilot will be two weeks. The work will be to document a new feature (from a prior release), using the specifications and other documents that were available when our team documented that feature. The FEATURENAME feature will be used for the pilot; this feature took three writers about four weeks to document. The pilot description will recommend that six writers be used by each vendor. Vendors will be paid for participation in the pilot, at a cost not to exceed $X.

One week after the end of the pilot, a conference call will be conducted with each vendor to review the content they submitted. The same personnel will participate in each call. The calls will be recorded. Additional conversations may be needed with one or more vendors. Within three weeks after the conclusion of the pilot, the vendor should be selected.

Depending on the level of confidence in the selected vendor, two vendors may be initially engaged, and the work split between them.

Section 5 – Negotiation, Contract Signing, and Budgeting: *[Plan for creating these deliverables.]*

After vendor selection, the Documentation Manager and the vendor will work together to create a startup plan and budget, as well as budgets and production targets for the first and second six-month periods. Also the contract will be negotiated and submitted for the approval and signature of the following stakeholders: *[list]*

Section 6 – Transition Plan: *[Details of the transition]*

After vendor selection, the Documentation Manager will travel to the offshore vendor's site for two weeks to train their team. Training areas to include: use of company laptops, VPN, technical writing software tools, and collaborative tools; company policies and communication protocols; rules for monitoring, tracking, and reporting; use of the style guide; authoring methodology; meeting participation; product training; and general orientation. Orientation will include a comprehensive introduction to our corporate culture and open discussion of two types of cultural differences and how they affect team collaboration: corporate culture and national culture.

During the visit, an assessment will be made of ongoing training needs. Communication and meeting participation plans will be adjusted as needed. Issues for exploration and resolution will be identified. During the second week, the offshore team will begin participating in some feature meetings and begin planning and writing topics.

Section 7 – Management, Reporting, and Evaluation: *[Details of how these tasks will be handled.]*

The offshore team will include a local manager/team lead, who will be the primary interface for project management communications. The following video calls will be scheduled:

- Weekly management calls
- Weekly all-team calls
- Weekly training/technical question calls

The training/technical question calls will occur whether or not specific training or questions have been planned in advance. These calls will in some cases be two hours or longer to accommodate planned trainings.

All members of the offshore team will track their activities hourly, including essential details such as topic identifier, activity, etc., using a tracking form agreed upon by management. A weekly activity and results report, including blocking issues and other issues, will submitted to management 24 hours before the management call. Blocking issues will be communicated immediately. Offshore IT support staff and onshore IT will join part of the management call at least monthly and will have additional IT calls as needed.

Section 8 – Processes, Editing, and Quality Control: *[Details of how these functions will be handled.]*

The offshore team will include at least one senior editor and other editing or quality control staff as needed. The initial staffing level will be determined after vendor selection. Editing and quality control staff will have calls with the Documentation Manager at least every two weeks. By the end of the second week, a review process will be agreed upon.

Section 9 – Ongoing Training and Travel: *[Planning and budget]*

Budgets will include at least one trip of two weeks duration every 12 months for the Documentation Manager or other onshore personnel to travel to the offshore site and train the offshore team. More frequent trips may be necessary. All-day training sessions can also be conducted remotely.

Section 10 – Key Success Factors, Risks/Pitfalls: *[Measures for evaluating success and issues.]*

Key success factors include:

- The initial plan requires approval by a sponsoring executive at least one level above all other stakeholders (for example, the CEO). This is to prevent abrupt changes due to stakeholder personnel change.
- Careful budgeting and frequent budget updates to all stakeholders.
- One-year budget approvals completed at least three months before the start of the annual budget period.
- In order to protect sunk investments, approvals must occur outside of the corporate budget schedule when needed.
- Changes to the success criteria must be approved by all stakeholders. Major changes, including any decision to cancel the entire engagement, must have a phase-in period of at least 60 days.
- Stakeholder personnel changes (for example due to reorganization, executive resignation, etc.), require an immediate (within four business days) comprehensive review by all stakeholders, including the sponsoring executive.

- Frequent quality assessments, process reviews, and productivity reviews – at least monthly in each case – must be shared with all stakeholders.

- Each team (offshore and onshore) must be flexible and willing to go the extra mile to resolve issues and problems.

- Work relationships must be established at the outset, via video meetings and other means. Team personnel changes require renewed focus on establishing relationships. Teams can invent creative ways to deepen and maintain relationships across continents.

Key risks or pitfalls to watch out for:

- Different holiday schedules in each country can disrupt work plans.

- Absences on either team can disrupt work plans.

- Misunderstandings can result when information is not confirmed. Meeting recordings, written meeting notes, and verbal confirmations are essential. ("I think you said blah blah blah. Did I get that right?")

- Cultural differences in behavior and communication can blindside members of both teams. The best way to deal with this is to ensure healthy, rich working relationships. Getting to know people well improves communication and understanding. Cultural awareness and training is also helpful. Curiosity about each other's culture is invaluable. Challenge team members to learn new things about their own cultural assumptions and attitudes by learning about the other culture.

- If team members are quick to blame, work relationships can deteriorate quickly. Training in accountability can help.

- Changing life-long habits or habits that span many generations is difficult and generally not successful in the absence of transformational education. One recommended source for such education is: http://www.landmarkworldwide.com[1]

- If we do not clearly document success criteria, quality criteria, and delivery and deadline details, misunderstandings can result that could lead to significant problems. Be careful not to rely on verbal communication alone, especially for important parameters.

---

[1] http://www.landmarkworldwide.com/

Section 11 – Implementation Timeline: *[Fill in with dates; the time frames shown in parentheses are suggestions to start with. The time required for each step will vary for every organization.]*

Table 12.2 – Implementation timeline

Event	Date
Plan approved	
Vendors to invite identified	
Competitive pilot instructions approved	
Vendors invited to participate in competitive pilot	
Participating vendors chosen	
(4 weeks for all of the above)	
Pilot begins	
Pilot ends (1-3 weeks)	
Initial pilot review calls with vendors complete (1 week)	
Vendor decision made and approved (2 weeks)	
Vendors notified of decision (immediate)	
Initial training trip scheduled (1 week)	
Startup plan and initial budget approved (1 week)	
Contract with vendor signed by both parties (1 week)	
Training trip begins (1 week)	

Event	Date
Training trip ends (1-2 weeks)	
Ramp-up efforts begin for offshore team (immediate)	
Weekly calls started (immediate)	
Monthly calls started (1-4 weeks)	
Monthly evaluations started (4 weeks)	
First quarterly business review (12-14 weeks)	
Second quarterly business review (12-14 weeks)	
Revised plan for second 6 months approved (2 weeks)	

Section 12 – Open questions, issues, areas to explore: *[Collect all of the TBD items and include them here.]*

- What is the role of accounting/CFO? At what points do we need to include them?
- Is offshore team travel to the onshore location feasible?
- What cross-team team-building is possible?
- If first-year quality and cost savings criteria are met, can training/travel budgets be increased?

CHAPTER 13
Sell Your Plan: Selling Up

If you're a documentation manager, you may feel frustrated with the lack of executive concern for content quality and the effectiveness of content in supporting organizational goals. In such a situation, it's crucial to understand what executives do care about most. Those concerns can provide an entry into their world. If executives are primarily focused on cost cutting, you can work to get ahead of them on that.

The same is true when it comes to outsourcing. If you don't have a good understanding of upper management's priorities, ask.

You can also learn by observing management communications and behavior. Be willing to challenge your assumptions. You may find areas of alignment, even if your managers do not prioritize your most important concerns.

Remember context, too. Sometimes management does not see things the way that you do because they lack context. Is there a relatively painless way that you can educate them about the context of your concerns? (See the section titled "Becoming an intrapreneur" in Chapter 14.)

At the same time, be careful not to oversell potential cost savings or to agree with exaggerated estimates of expected cost savings, even if management seems committed to them. While pay scales can vary up to 10 times between offshore and onshore personnel, given the other factors involved in outsourcing, savings over 60% are unlikely to materialize (and if they do, they're unlikely to last over time). See Chapter 9 for more on this topic.

Make sure you understand the expectations of upper management and other stakeholders. It is crucial that executives and managers are clear about the potential costs, benefits, and timelines of potential outsourcing efforts. Managers should understand that launching an outsourcing effort involves significant upfront costs for travel, training, and management support and that cost savings may not be fully realized for several years. Moreover, functions that were previously less important may become crucial. For example, if your organization does not currently employ editors, you may discover they are essential when you add writers whose first language is not English.

Outsourcing success also depends upon consistent funding. For example, if upper management approves the outsourcing plan, but does not approve funding for travel, training, editing, and additional management, good outcomes are unlikely.

Given the frequency of organizational change in most enterprises, your plan – and the commitment to funding the details of that plan – must be able to survive personnel changes at the top. Ask your manager to seek an ongoing commitment (including time and money) to the outsourcing plan from higher-level managers. If necessary, help educate these stakeholders to make sure they can address concerns that go beyond cost.

Just as with other aspects of leadership, the most important word in working with upper management is: listen. Listen for what is not being said and focus on finding common points of inspiration. You may find that what inspires the executive team will also inspire you

CHAPTER 14
Sell Your Plan: Selling Down

Many executives and managers do not understand the necessity of selling change, especially controversial change. They act as if they can simply hand down edicts and tell employees "That's the way it is." But employees need – and deserve – more than that. Most employees want to feel good about their employers and their work situation. By engaging them in the process of change, you give them a much greater opportunity to contribute to the success of your organization. If you explain your decisions clearly – along with the rationale behind them – you are likely to find some support. However, if you don't allow anyone to challenge you, you may not get any authentic support.

The key word here is: listen. Explain the changes and listen to people's concerns. Approach conversations with curiosity and humility.

After all, you don't know everything. The people doing the work usually have a much more detailed understanding of what's involved. In the absence of clear communication and meaningful dialogue, however, they may also have misconceptions about what your planned changes will bring.

Your technical writers may be concerned that outsourcing will result in a reduction in content quality. There are several steps you can take to address this concern:

- Start the offshore writers off with easier tasks and simpler content to work with. This can yield multiple benefits:
  - Offshore writers will have a greater chance of initial success.
  - Onshore writers will be freed up from tasks that are less interesting to them.
  - Onshore writers can focus on more advanced work.
  - Morale may improve for onshore writers.
- Depending on your team structure, you can assign an existing writer to partner with one or more offshore writers. This can help improve both content quality and team collaboration.

■ Use your knowledge of your team to choose the best offshore partners for each, perhaps with the help of the offshore manager. Is there one team member who has been most resistant to outsourcing? Perhaps you can partner that person with the most senior or most skilled person on the offshore team.

Technical writers may also fear losing their jobs. Don't give them false hope, but usually there are truthful things you can say that will reduce their fear or make it more manageable.

In many cases, outsourcing does not result in layoffs at all, or there are very limited staff reductions. However, in almost all cases where managers do not share their staffing plans, some staff will be severely affected by their fear of job loss. They may become more resistant to change, and you may even lose the people you most want to keep.

Complete transparency is not always optimal. That said, complete opacity is rarely required and is usually detrimental.

Adjusting to outsourcing as a team member

Staff attitudes also matter. In hiring, attitude factors account for 90% of success, and the same is true of challenging transitions. In an organization that is considering outsourcing, personnel at all levels may need to think about how to sell themselves, how to demonstrate their value, and how to contribute effectively in a new organizational structure. The next two sections discuss this mindset; you may wish to share these sections with your technical writing team and other staff.

Becoming an intrapreneur

Regardless of your role at your organization, you can be most effective if you commit yourself to acting as an intrapreneur – someone who uses entrepreneurial skills to create or transform products, services, structures, or processes. You know your organization: now how can you make it better?

As an intrapreneur, you will face the same challenges that confront anyone who seeks to change an organization: Can you make a difference? Can you have a positive impact on something much larger than yourself?

The key to addressing these challenges successfully is to realize that the question, "Can I make a difference?" is a spiritual question, not a logical question. You can assemble a mountain of data to argue either side of the question. You can convince yourself, if you choose, that there is nothing you can do. In fact, you probably know at least one person who, in the face of a big challenge, has said, "There's nothing I can do." Perhaps that person is you.

You can also convince yourself, if you choose, that you *can* have a positive impact.

When I say that "Can I make a difference?" is a spiritual question, I'm not talking about traditional religion. Instead, I'm talking about spiritual awareness – your relationship with yourself and your commitment to personal growth and change.

Each of us has the ability, in cooperation with others, to become an historical actor – someone who effects change in institutions or in society as a whole. Yet many people do not think of themselves as capable of causing change. This is largely because trillions of dollars have been spent to convince us that our primary role in life is to be a consumer.

If you buy this car, you will be happy. (In other words, we're not interested in your opinion, or your innovative contribution; we just want your money.)

Capitalism has many benefits, of course, but capitalism can also create disempowered individuals, people who have no awareness of their power as independent, creative social actors. The good news is, you can develop this awareness. You don't have to overthrow the system to get in touch with your ability to participate creatively and actively in organizational change. You only need to see yourself as an intrapreneur and act as one.

Switching perspectives

How can you be effective as an intrapreneur? The key is to be able to switch perspectives. Think about the decision-makers or staff that you will need on your side in order to move your organization in a positive direction. What are their needs, concerns, and priorities? What do they care about most? How do they make decisions? What kinds of information do they tend to notice or listen to most intently? What pressures are they under? What has sold them on new ideas in the past? What has turned them against new ideas?

In some cases you may not have access to the decision-maker, or you may have access but that person does not listen to what you have to say. This is where networking and developing relationships with others can help. Who are your allies? Can one of your allies help you gain access or be heard? Can they be your champion, inviting you into the inner circle, coaching you on how to present information and win over key decision-makers?

Before anyone else can be your champion, however, you must believe in yourself.

Establishing trust

In the absence of a relationship with management built on mutual trust, it is easy for workers – even accomplished professionals – to fall into an attitude of mistrust and disloyalty. This attitude can lead very quickly to behaviors that amount to sabotage.[1]

One of the basic commitments that I require from my staff is loyalty. I am clear that I do not want blind loyalty. I need people to speak up, to challenge management. The commitment of loyalty means that they give the company and the management the benefit of the doubt. When they notice something that bothers them, instead of gossiping about it with others or keeping it to themselves – where it can corrode their morale and attitude – they must bring it to management or human resources. They must give the company a chance to address their concern. After that, if they feel we are not address-

---

[1] See *Sabotage in the American Workplace: Anecdotes of Dissatisfaction, Mischief and Revenge,* edited by Martin Sprouse.

ing it properly, we encourage them to report us to the appropriate author-ities. But they must first communicate with us.

If you discourage people from speaking up and challenging management's plans, you can expect that you will get some disloyalty. When management doesn't listen, it is very easy for morale to deteriorate to the point where people who once loved the company end up sabotaging it from within.

The power of authentic listening is immense. Even if your plans are quite detrimental to some of your staff's futures, actively seeking out and listening to their concerns and feedback can have an enormously positive impact on the cooperation you receive.

Why do some people think outsourcing won't work? Perhaps they have negative past experiences with outsourcing. But perhaps the problem is more basic: they're used to being ignored and devalued. You can fix that.

CHAPTER 15

Stage a Pilot

A pilot is a small project that enables you to test an outsourcing vendor or situation. No matter how carefully you've researched and planned your outsourcing, you cannot predict exactly how things will go.

Staging a pilot allows you to get a better idea of the issues that may arise. You can observe what works well and what doesn't. You can also devise plans for improvement, all at a lower cost and risk level than a full production scenario entails.

When planning a pilot, consider these questions:

- **Will this pilot be paid or unpaid?** Most vendors are only willing to do unpaid pilots if the scope of work is very small – perhaps 1-3 person-days of work, maximum. However, for many situations a larger pilot is needed to get a clear sense of the vendor's capabilities. It may take a day or two just for the initial orientation and research, before actual work on the pilot project can begin.
- **Will this be a competitive pilot?** In a competitive pilot, several different vendors are given the same set of work to accomplish. Typically competitive pilots are paid, as the amount of work is significant. Generally, competitive pilots make sense for larger projects and/or ongoing work. While competitive pilots pose a higher upfront cost, they can provide significant benefits and savings down the road. If a vendor is a poor match for your needs, ending the relationship early can save you a great deal of money, time, and frustration later on.

Pilots versus RFPs

While pilot projects have few downsides, Requests for Proposals (RFPs) can be counterproductive. Nevertheless, some companies require them.

First, let's define our terms. The use of terms in this area varies widely across industries and companies. Do not expect your company or another company to define these terms the same way I do. In this book, I use these working definitions:

- **Pilot, or Pilot Project:** A small project (usually one month or less, for a team of between one and ten people) that a new vendor undertakes to demonstrate their capabilities and value. Pilots can be paid or unpaid and competitive or non-competitive.

- **Proof of Concept (POC):** A small project that a new vendor undertakes to demonstrate that their proposed solution to your problems will work.

- **Request for Proposal (RFP):** A formal document your company creates that specifies the parameters required for vendor proposals for a specific project or engagement. RFPs can include detailed information and requirements, detailed application forms or other forms, and any other criteria you desire.

- **Request for Quote (RFQ):** A formal document your company creates that specifies the parameters required for vendor estimates for a specific project or engagement.

- **Request for Information (RFI):** A formal document your company creates that requests specific information from each of a variety of vendors you are considering. The information may relate to vendor capabilities, corporate structure, history, etc. It may include resumes or summary information about their staff, standard rates, fees, and charges, and similar information.

When you send out an RFP or RFQ, you are asking a vendor to create a plan to meet your organization's needs and goals. Typically, vendors are poorly positioned to do so, because they lack a deep understanding of your organization's culture, processes, and concerns. Regardless of how much information or orientation you provide, it is difficult for vendors to play catch-up in a short timeframe.

RFPs and RFQs entail significant investments of funds and resources for vendors, usually with no guarantee of a return. Unlike pilots, which can be paid, most RFPs and RFQs do not offer any payment for proposal/quote development and submission.

Making your RFP/RFQ process simple and quick can encourage vendor participation and earn you a more diverse pool of vendor applicants. However, if your RFP or RFQ is not detailed, vendors will likely end up playing a guessing game as they assemble their proposals. In an effort to avert favoritism or corruption, some companies also limit communication between vendors and those who will review submissions. This can backfire, because the vendors who are best at guessing what you mean and what you want may not be the best at delivering what you really need.

Should you use a simple RFP or RFQ that leads to a more diverse pool of vendor applicants, yet may result in confusing or inappropriate proposals? Or should you lean toward a complex, detailed document, which may turn off your best vendor candidates?

One solution is to combine a fairly simple RFP with a competitive pilot. Vendors respond to the RFP if they wish to participate in the pilot. The RFP explains the pilot project requirements. Vendors who are not capable of completing the pilot, or not confident in their ability to do so, may choose not to participate. The RFP itself may involve a short list of questions. Based on the answers – as well as any additional discussions you choose to have with each vendor – you then choose which vendors will compete in the pilot project.

This scenario is more appealing to well-qualified vendors, because the pilot allows them to actually demonstrate their capabilities to you.

Think carefully about these questions before starting a pilot:

- How large (team size and duration) does the pilot need to be to give you enough work to perform an adequate evaluation of the vendor's capabilities?
- Will the pilot be paid or unpaid? It is reasonable to expect a vendor to perform perhaps 1-3 person-days of work for free, particularly if they have already made your short list. More than that should be paid for.

- Will it be a competitive pilot? Inviting two or more vendors to perform the same tasks can give you a good idea of the value each vendor offers. How do their rates compare to their quality? How well can you communicate with each vendor? What issues do you anticipate with each vendor? What is it like working with each vendor on the pilot?

Remember that the best work results from a win-win situation in which the vendor is able to do good work, be responsive to your needs, make a decent profit, and invest in their staff so they can continue to deliver quality content. Doing a lot of work for free is not a sustainable business model.

Once you've chosen your preferred vendor, and they've accomplished an initial project to your satisfaction, consider whether you really need a proposal for the next project. Often it works better to get off the proposal treadmill and develop less formal and more effective methods of collaborative project planning. On the other hand, if your assessment of the vendor's performance is less than stellar, you may want to use an RFP to ensure that the satisfaction criteria for the next project are crystal clear, and that the vendor knows they are still under the microscope.

CHAPTER 16

Get Started: Kick-off, Training, and Travel

Once you have selected your vendor, signed contracts, and agreed on a roll-out plan, a good way to get started is to have one or more key persons travel to the offshore location to meet and train the new team. In most cases this offers the best chances for ongoing success and is worth far more than its cost.

There are also other options. One or more key people from the vendor can visit your offices, meet your staff, and undergo training. Sessions can be recorded via video or audio, and some sessions can include offshore personnel virtually. After returning offshore, the vendor's staff can then provide further on-site training to their offshore colleagues. One word of caution, however: travel to your country may be difficult for offshore personnel due to visa issues.

For most projects, some kind of travel is essential for a successful kick-off. Do not underestimate the value of in-person interactions in forming effective working relationships. Working remotely with people you have met is far different from working remotely with people you've never met.

Training

What training do you provide to new, onshore writers? Offshore writers should receive the same training as your in-house writers. In addition, they should receive training to address new processes, remote locations and work times, lack of cultural familiarity, etc.

Remember, your onshore team has relatively easy, immediate access to people in your office who can help with questions and obstacles. Because your offshore teams don't have these advantages, they need more training time and clearly identified support channels.

Be sure to include the following two types of cultural issues in your training:

- **Corporate culture:** The new team needs to learn as much as possible about the culture of your organization. Learning about rules, procedures, processes, organization charts, and the like is a good start. Add some discussion of how things get done, how decisions get made, and how planning happens in your organization and in theirs.
- **Regional/national culture:** Culture shock and culture clash can cause significant problems. The key to success is for everyone to be committed to cultural learning and to getting to know each other as individuals. Be interested in their culture and encourage them to be interested in yours. Explore the differences, especially the ways that cultural differences affect the office environment and the work. How is conflict handled? Who asks questions of whom? How are key English words used, for example: yes, no, agreed, maybe, etc.

Your initial training sessions can help form effective team relationships. Your goal should be to make the offshore team full members of the overall team. Healthy relationships fuel learning, reduce dysfunction, and increase productivity. Without healthy relationships, learning becomes difficult.

Building relationships needs to be an ongoing effort. Seek to create opportunities for team building, despite the challenges of geography. The impact on productivity and the effective resolution of issues can be quite dramatic.

CHAPTER 17
Set up Structures

Once you've got your offshore team up and running, don't allow your focus to be entirely eaten up by putting out fires. Institute some regular check-in points when the entire team can assess progress, acknowledge and learn from what's working well, and acknowledge and learn from what isn't.

A commitment to continuous process improvement is essential to outsourcing success. Your processes should include regular monitoring, evaluation, and course-correction components.

Outsourcing is a large business change. There will inevitably be issues, situations, and problems that no one anticipated. When these arise, approach them with curiosity, humility, and a commitment to collaborative innovation. If you did a good job of setting up the outsourcing situation initially, most problems along the way will be solvable.

It's important to identify potential problems early, however. Regular reports and measures can help. In discussing problems, be careful not to jump too quickly to solutions. Spend time defining the problem and identifying its root causes. If you haven't correctly identified what the real problem is, you're unlikely to solve it.

That said, there are situations where you must abandon ship or dramatically change course and sacrifice your sunk costs. Don't move to this stage lightly – be sure that you first understand the root causes of the problem and explore solutions with all stakeholders.

You may want to institute a quarterly or annual business review, with the participation of managers or executives from both your organization and the vendor. This can be done virtually, or it can be done partially virtually, where at least one person travels to be present with the other team during the meetings.

Staying informed

What kinds of regular reports do you need? Start with your current, onshore reporting system. Consider your goals. If you are working with an outsourced vendor, you'll want to gather enough information, in enough detail, to justify ongoing expenses to both your accounting department and executives. For example, what did each offshore writer do for eight hours each day? What topics did they work on and for how long? Are your offshore writers asking questions and seeking to understand your business more fully? If not, why not? What other information will help you in assessing effectiveness, productivity, and quality?

As you gain more experience, you'll develop a better understanding of what you need to measure and track and how best to do so.

Milestones and metrics

You can learn a lot by tracking a vendor's success in hitting deadlines – meeting specific milestones that are identified in advance. You can also learn a great deal by using specific measures on a daily or less frequent basis. Here are some examples of measures you can use:

- Cost per page or per topic
- Pages or topics produced per week
- Errors per page or per topic (broken down by error type)
- Responsiveness to requests, changes, questions, by both parties (e.g., percent of issues responded to within 24 hours)

For any of these measures, you can begin measuring your local team's performance before you start outsourcing. This gives you a baseline that you can compare to the results from outsourcing. Remember, supporting outsourcing will change the dynamics of your local team, so once you start, it will be difficult to establish a clear baseline.

Your findings can be useful in maintaining internal support. For example, can you show that using an outsourced team led to 35% more content produced per week and cost 15% less than expanding the local team? See Chapter 9 for more details on how to compare costs.

Case Studies and Conclusion

CHAPTER 18
Case Studies

Every situation, every company, and every team is different. Throughout this book, I've tried to cover all the bases – to provide specifics, but also general guidelines. In this section, I provide three actual case studies from our experience working with clients at Saiff Solutions to show some of the guidelines in action. Although I have omitted names and identifying details, I've tried to stick to the facts of each situation. However, we can rarely see any situation from more than our own vantage point. Any inaccuracies are due to errors in my memory, knowledge, or judgement about each situation.

Case Study 1: Despite management changes, you can achieve success with the right partner

A software division of a large Asian conglomerate, located primarily in the US but with software development teams in the Philippines, had a very experienced, competent technical writing staff in the US. Their workload was growing and capacity was an issue. While overall process maturity was high, they were saddled with an outdated and cumbersome Component Content Management System (CCMS).

For many years, they had an experienced documentation and localization manager who worked diligently to establish a relationship with Saiff Solutions before she retired. Afterwards, several documentation managers came and went. They were based in a US city whose location made it difficult to attract and keep both managers and writers.

We were asked to do a one-month pilot project with one offshore technical writer. The project went very well. Two months later, we started a larger project, updating documentation for a major software release. At that time, we had fewer than five full-time staff, so we added several new people to the project, including six technical writers and one graphic designer.

Our team in the Philippines worked with onshore staff in the US and also with in-house staff located in a different city in the Philippines. Except for one brief trip to that city by two of our team members, all training was done remotely. The development team in the Philippines had little experience working with technical writers. However, the trip made a difference in establishing good work relationships, and all three teams cooperated well together during the entire 5-month project. The US writing team did peer editing. We used our own editor, and the content was edited again by US writers. Our team also had a team lead.

The US writing team appointed one of their senior members as the project lead and primary contact with our offshore team. This US project lead and our team lead in the Philippines were in daily contact by email or phone. That relationship was key to the success of the project.

The project was completed on time, with good quality. The US team was very pleased with the results. Plans were hatched for work on the next release to start within a month. However, the company had a delay in getting upper management approval for the second project. By the time the project started, there were only two months available to do a similar amount of work as the first 5-month project.

Because our team had learned from the first project, we needed to add only two additional technical writers to meet the shortened deadline. The client was very happy with our work.

During the previous year, the US team had been through several managers. After the end of the second large project, the US team finally got an experienced manager who was committed to staying with them long term. She was able to transition them to a better CCMS, which resulted in a significant increase in the US team's efficiency, reducing the need for extra capacity. She maintained a good relationship with us and has been in touch recently to discuss upcoming needs.

Lessons learned

Management is crucial in all locations. This includes more than formal managers. In this case, it was the leaders one level down from management, in both the US and the Philippines, who made everything work. Choosing the right outsourcing partner, and having strong leaders and teams in all locations, can make success possible even in the midst of frequent management changes.

Case Study 2: Good management leads to good results, for as long as it does

A large global consulting company had a software division spread between several US locations and Manila, Philippines. This included an experienced team of US technical writers, some employees and some contractors, led by a very capable and experienced documentation manager. The division used the Agile Scrum development methodology. Their process maturity was high, and their tools supported their activities well.

The work was expanding beyond the capacity of the US writing team. Most of the development and QA teams were located in Manila. Efforts to hire technical writers directly in Manila had not borne fruit. The documentation manager spent over a year getting to know Saiff Solutions as a potential offshore vendor in the Philippines. He understood that even if the company could hire technical writers in Manila, they lacked the local management to support the writers. He did not want to move to Manila, even temporarily, so he focused on getting approval for an outsourcing engagement.

An agreement was signed for three of our writers and one editor to start ongoing work. These four team members used company laptops and, via the company VPN, accessed all of the resources that other team members used. They visited the office in Manila periodically and participated in other meetings remotely. They were tightly integrated into the Scrum teams.

At the start of the project, the documentation manager visited our team in the Philippines for two weeks of training. The training covered company orientation, policies, work standards, styles, tools, resources, and product training. This two week trip proved invaluable to the success of the project.

There were some interpersonal issues between the teams. Initially one of the US writers had difficulty supporting our writers. Some of the Manila client staff were resistant to the idea of outsourcing. However, due to excellent management support from the documentation manager and a robust communications flow, these obstacles were overcome.

The engagement proceeded well, and the company was quite pleased with the results. In addition to meeting quality metrics, the goal of having one offshore writer support more than one feature team was achieved in the first six months. After seven months, the company, as a result of a merger and other organizational changes, cancelled the contract with us and also laid off their entire in-house writing team.

Lessons learned

Process maturity matters. Agile teams can work together effectively across continents. Cultural and personality issues can be resolved with good management.

Case Study 3: Leadership and trust can lead to success

A division of a large Japanese conglomerate that manufactures heavy machinery had a plant with 1,000 workers in the Philippines. They had market dominance in China and Japan, where their maintenance and repair documentation was provided in Chinese and Japanese. To serve new markets, they needed good documentation in English.

As is true of many Japanese companies, they had no experience as a company with technical writing. A common approach in Japan is to assume that if a Japanese engineer writes the documentation in Japanese, and a translator translates that documentation into English, good English documentation is the result. In practice, that is rarely the case. Neither engineers nor translators have expertise in designing usable documentation.

This company was fortunate to have an executive who had worked for 25 years in the US for a large technology firm. He had been exposed to technical writing there. He also had the idea that, due to the prevalence of English and the lower labor costs, the Philippines was a good place to find technical writing help. So they searched for and found Saiff Solutions.

I visited Japan several times each year to work directly with both the engineers and the machinery. We used photos, videos, recordings, and notes, as well as both in-person and virtual training, to support the writing team.

The writing team also visited the company plant, which is in another city in the Philippines, approximately once per year. Because that plant worked on components, no fully assembled machines were available there to work with. Despite that limitation, during the last phase of the project they sent some of their engineers to visit us, which was less costly than having me travel to Japan.

While email was certainly effective, conference calls or video calls were of limited help due to the limited English skills of the engineers.

Over approximately two years, our small writing team (two to three writers) produced almost two dozen manuals. The company primarily used outdated software and was reluctant to try new tools. They were extremely security-conscious, but we were able to develop a relationship with them based on trust. We persuaded them to switch from Word to Framemaker, but the change did not stick. Process improvements such as topic-based authoring and documentation governance were out of reach.

The company was very pleased with our work. Business changes and budget cuts led to that work stopping, but they are still hoping to get approval for us to help them in the future.

Lessons learned

Individuals matter. Occasional in-person meetings can make a tremendous positive difference and can overcome significant language and cultural barriers.

Summary

Every company, project, work environment, and situation is different. In business, change is frequent. Relationships require both resiliency and stability in the face of change.

Having the best methodologies and controls for project management and vendor management does not eliminate the impact of the human element. Business relationships always occur between people.

Outsourcing introduces complexities and challenges that are difficult, if not impossible, to navigate successfully without effective, frequent communication and trust. Think about how you will build and maintain trust.

Companies focus on stability, and they often use the size of a business as a measure of stability. Yet, the largest organizations often experience tremendous instability. All of the guidelines and metrics in the world cannot help you when the magnitude of change makes prior measurements and plans irrelevant. Yet, developing good relationships can help you through difficult times.

CHAPTER 19
Conclusion

We are now entering a golden age of technical communication. There are technical writers working in dozens of countries, many with over ten years' experience in topic-based authoring and DITA.

To many technical communicators, the idea of outsourcing technical writing is still quite threatening. Nonetheless, the evidence is clear: outsourcing technical writing can result in improved quality, improved processes, improved morale for everyone, and reduced costs.

Myths about outsourcing persist. One of the most damaging myths is the idea that outsourcing can reduce costs by 80% or even 90%. Clearly, when outsourcing is planned and managed well, significant cost savings are possible over time. But these savings are not automatic, and they are not instantaneous.

Like most things in business and life, successful outsourcing requires a lot of careful thinking and hard work. When outsourcing is poorly conceived, planned, and executed, it can amplify an organization's worst tendencies. When outsourcing is done well, however, it can help an organization grow and thrive.

APPENDIX A
Sample Contract

This appendix contains a sample technical writing agreement. As with any agreement, you should always retain your own legal counsel to review the applicability of this contract to your unique situation.

> The author and the publisher of this book provide this sample on an "as is" basis, without warranty. The author and XML Press shall have neither liability nor responsibility to any person or entity with respect to any loss or damages arising from the information contained in this sample contract.

TECHNICAL WRITING MASTER SERVICE AGREEMENT

Agreement between COMPANY, a COUNTRY corporation with a place of business at ADDRESS, and VENDOR, a COUNTRY corporation with a place of business at ADDRESS. VENDOR will provide technical writing, graphic design, motion graphics, consulting or related services for COMPANY.

Services to be Provided and Conditions Thereof:

(1) VENDOR will write and edit documentation or other content, perform file conversions, reformatting, graphic design, or other related tasks as requested by CLIENT.

(2) Confidentiality: In the course of the performance of this agreement, one party ("Discloser") may disclose or provide the other party ("Recipient") access to, or may come into possession of, materials and information, orally or in written documentation which may contain confidential and/or proprietary information of Discloser, its customers or prospective customers or its vendors or prospective vendors ("Confidential Information"); provided that Confidential Information does not include information which is (a) already known to Recipient without obligation of confidentiality, (b) is or later becomes publicly available through no wrongful act of Recipient, (c) available from a third party under no obligation of confidentiality, or (d)

independently developed by Recipient without reliance on Discloser's Confidential Information. Recipient agrees to keep the Confidential Information confidential and not use the Confidential Information for any purposes other than in connection with the Agreement. Recipient agrees to take all reasonable security measures and other precautions, including no less than those it takes to protect its own proprietary or confidential information, to prevent any disclosure of any Confidential Information to any third party. Recipient shall also limit access to the Information within its own organization to those employees to whom disclosure is necessary for purposes of the Agreement. These restrictions will not apply to any disclosure of Confidential Information to the extent required by court or regulatory order provided that Recipient gives prompt notice of such an order to Discloser and cooperates, at Discloser's expense, in preventing and/or limiting such disclosure.

(3) CLIENT recognizes that VENDOR cannot competently perform its work without access to information and (in some cases) software that only CLIENT can provide. CLIENT agrees to provide access and information as needed for VENDOR to perform its tasks, and to answer questions in a timely manner, with initial responses within 2 business days.

(4) VENDOR will provide interim drafts for review by CLIENT. CLIENT will provide review comments in a timely manner. CLIENT understands that without adequate CLIENT feedback, VENDOR cannot produce quality content.

(5) CLIENT will pay VENDOR based upon the time spent by VENDOR personnel on CLIENT's projects, as follows (all rates in $US): $X per hour for Technical Writers, $X per hour for Technical Illustrators, $X per hour for Team Leads and Quality Control Specialists, $X per hour for Technical Editors, $X per hour for Senior Technical Editors, and $X per hour for Project Managers.

(6) Projects: This contract covers a variety of projects, as agreed upon between CLIENT and VENDOR.

(7) VENDOR will invoice CLIENT monthly. CLIENT will pay within 30 days from receipt of invoice via wire transfer to BANKING INFORMA-TION.

(8) Contract termination: Either party may terminate this contract with 30 calendar days' written notice.

(9) Jurisdiction: Any dispute arising under this contract will be resolved by the courts of CITY, STATE/PROVINCE, COUNTRY.

By signing below, parties agree to this Agreement's terms, effective on the date of the last signature below.

VENDOR   CLIENT

By: _____   By: _____

Date: _____   Date: _____

Print name and title

_____   _____

Colophon

About the Author

Barry Saiff is a leading expert in technical writing outsourcing and managing technical writers. Barry has experienced technical writing outsourcing from both sides: as a tech comm leader in the USA and as a manager of offshore technical writers and customer liaison in the Philippines. After 26 years developing software documentation for some of the largest US companies, Barry moved to the Philippines to found Saiff Solutions (saiffsolutions.com).

Barry frequently leads webinars and speaks at conferences. His popular 7 Habits series of blogs, infographics, and webinars has been featured by the Society for Technical Communication. His company has developed technical content for some of the world's largest corporations.

Barry holds a bachelor of arts in anthropology from Princeton and a master of arts in international affairs from American University.

About the Content Wrangler Content Strategy Book Series

The Content Wrangler Content Strategy Book Series from XML Press provides content professionals with a road map for success. Each volume provides practical advice, best practices, and lessons learned from the most knowledgeable content strategists in the world. Visit the companion website for more information contentstrategybooks.com.

About XML Press

XML Press (xmlpress.net) was founded in 2008 to publish content that helps technical communicators be more effective. Our publications support managers, social media practitioners, technical communicators, and content strategists and the engineers who support their efforts.

Our publications are available through most retailers, and discounted pricing is available for volume purchases for educational or promotional use. For more information, send email to orders@xmlpress.net or call us at (970) 231-3624.